D0897829

ENGLISH EMBLEM BOOKS

No. 11

Selected and Edited by

JOHN HORDEN

Introductory Note by

KARL JOSEF HÖLTGEN

Henry Hawkins

The Devout Hart
1634

THE SCOLAR PRESS

1975

ISBN 0 85967 258 1

Published and printed in Great Britain by
The Scolar Press Limited, 59-61 East Parade,
Ilkley, Yorkshire and
39 Great Russell Street,
London WC1

NOTE

Reproduced (original size) by permission of the Provost and Fellows of Eton College; pressmark: C.a.7.8. This interesting copy includes both the original title-leaf, dated 1634, and a printed cancel slip which reads 'M. DC. XXXVIII.'. The cancel slip has been carefully cut to size to fit the lower section of the title-page in order to alter only the date. It has not been pasted onto the title-page, as was obviously intended, but has been bound in like a small leaf. In this facsimile it has been reproduced on a separate leaf preceding the title-page to show that page both in its original and its proposed states. The Eton copy of *The Devout Hart* is the only one known to have the emblem plates, although even here two of the engravings have not been printed: the plates for 'the Heavenly Nuptials in the hart', p. [253], and 'the mirrour of the hart', p. [287], are wanting. Accordingly, the corresponding plates, 19 (facing p. 176) and 20 (facing p. 199), of Etienne Luzvic's *Cor Deo Devotum*, (Frankfort) 1722, have been included as an Appendix. They are taken from the British Library copy (pressmark: 4412.e.21), and are reproduced by permission of the British Library Board. The plates of this later edition were engraved by a Nuremberg engraver of the early eighteenth century who signed himself M. Nunzer.

The Devout Hart or Royal Throne of the Pacifical Salomon was published by Jean Cousturier at Rouen in 1634. The title contains a biblical allusion: 'Moreover, the king [Solomon] made a great throne of ivory, and overlaid it with best gold' (1 Kings 10, 18; Authorized Version). The meaning becomes clear especially through the series of emblematic plates. Christ, a second Solomon, makes a new throne for himself in the devout heart of the Christian (cf. pp. 111–13). In catalogues and bibliographies the book is usually listed under Luzvic, the author of the French original (v. *STC* 17001; Allison and Rogers 483 and 484). It can now be stated with assurance that the English translator, who on page 6 signs the dedication with the initials H. A., is the Jesuit Henry Hawkins, who wrote *Partheneia Sacra*, 1633 (also published by Cousturier at Rouen), and who translated or adapted six other books. From 1632 he used the initials H. A. instead of H. H. in four of his works, probably for reasons of greater safety. On account of these initials he has been confused with Henry Annesley, another Catholic writer (v. Wolfgang Lottes, 'Henry Annesley: a Recusant's Progress from Oxfordshire to Bavaria', *Anglia*, 91, 1973). Authoritative Jesuit bibliographers, Alegambe, Southwell, and De Backer-Sommervogel, fail to include *The Devout Hart* in Hawkins' canon, but their information is sometimes incomplete (they also missed his translation of La Serre's *The Sweete Thoughts of Death, and Eternity*, Allison and Rogers 441), and in the present instance Hawkins was only one of four Jesuit authors who had a hand in the several stages of the work. The circumstances of publication and its affinities with the rest of Hawkins' works, especially *Partheneia Sacra*, leave no reasonable doubt that he was responsible for *The Devout Hart*. Rosemary Freeman, in *English Emblem Books*, 1948, was the first to establish his claim.

Partheneia Sacra and *The Devout Hart* are the only English Recusant emblem books and are both important examples of the fusion of emblem and meditation. *Ashrea: or The Grove of Beatitudes* by E. M., which is sometimes classed with these two (cf. Freeman, *op. cit.*), may be regarded as the third English Catholic emblem book (although this is not absolutely certain, its author being unidentified), but it is not a Recusant book because it was published openly in London in 1665. It is also a little outside the main stream of the emblematic and meditative traditions (v. John Horden's Note to *Ashrea*, Scolar

Press, English Emblem Books series, No. 18, 1970). Of Hawkins' two emblem books, *Partheneia Sacra* shows the greater artistry of prose, originality of subject matter, and inventiveness in the design of the emblematic structure. *The Devout Hart*, however, can claim attention as the English representative of the series of emblems on the heart known as *Cor Iesu amanti sacrum* by Anton Wierix. This series was extremely widespread and popular on the Continent because it expressed and, at the same time, helped to shape the fervent spirit of seventeenth-century devotion. The importance of *The Devout Hart* has not been recognised because copies are very rare and it has never before been reprinted. Indeed, it has only come to light recently that one copy, at Eton, preserves the emblematic engravings which were clearly part of the original design but somehow failed to appear in the other known copies. Allison and Rogers, in *A Catalogue of Catholic Books in English printed abroad or secretly in England 1558–1640*, 1956, record a second copy of the 1638 reissue at Heythrop College, but in 1973 the Librarian of that College, now part of the University of London, reported that he did not hold the work in any edition. Only three copies of *The Devout Hart* seem to be known at present, including one at Ushaw College not listed by Allison and Rogers.

A short account of Hawkins' life will be found in my Note to *Partheneia Sacra*, Scolar Press, English Emblem Books series, No. 10, 1971. Since then have appeared Josephine E. Secker's article, 'Henry Hawkins, S.J., 1577–1646: a Recusant Writer and Translator of the Early Seventeenth Century', *Recusant History*, 11, 1972, and Wolfgang Lottes' published dissertation, *Henry Hawkins. Leben und Werk eines englischen Jesuiten des 17. Jahrhunderts*, Erlangen, 1974, a full study with some important discoveries. Descended from an old family of Catholic gentry, Henry Hawkins was the second son of

Sir Thomas Hawkins, of Nash Court, Kent. A glimpse of Henry's face can be caught in the parish church of Boughton-under-Blean on the family monument by the Recusant sculptor Epiphanius Evesham, who executed work of great artistic merit for a number of Catholic families (v. the photographs in K. A. Esdaile, *English Church Monuments 1580 to 1840*, 1946, plate 9; E. Mercer, *Oxford History of English Art*, 1962, plate 89b; W. Lottes, *op. cit.*, plate 1). The year of Henry's birth had always been given wrongly until evidence of his baptism on 8 October 1577 was produced (v. my Note to *Partheneia Sacra, op. cit.*). As a boy Henry would have received private tuition, and the name of Mr. Greene, Recusant schoolmaster in his father's house about 1587–89, survives among the Hussey Manuscripts at Lambeth Palace (1587–89, ff. 19–20; cf. 'A Biographical Catalogue of Catholic Schoolmasters', *Recusant History*, 7, 1963–64). The impression gathered from his books, that Hawkins was learned, well-educated, and thoroughly at home in the Elizabethan cultural milieu, is confirmed by Dr. Lottes' discovery of his Oxford matriculation entry, which has escaped all previous biographers (v. A. Clark, *Register of the University of Oxford*, II, ii, 192; J. Foster, *Alumni Oxonienses*, II, p. 676). In 1592, at the age of fourteen, Hawkins went to Gloucester Hall, a college then favoured by Catholics and already attended by his elder brother Thomas. Thomas Hawkins, from 1618 Sir Thomas, was also a prolific writer, as were other members of the family. His best-known work, a translation of Caussin's *Holy Court*, a kind of conduct book, came originally (1626) as a Recusant publication from the press of the English Jesuit College of S. Omer but was later reprinted in London. Like his brother Henry, Sir Thomas tended to address his dedications to members of the Catholic nobility, and both brothers may at times have enjoyed the protection of influential courtiers. The example of the Hawkins family confirms the general impression that the strictness of punitive measures against Recusants varied considerably with time, place, circumstances, social position, and connections. Henry is next heard of at Rome in 1609 when he entered the English College. After ordination and further study he became a member of the Society of Jesus in Flanders in 1615, went to England and was banished soon after his arrival in 1618. He returned and worked in secret as a missionary for about twenty-five years. He died on 18 August 1646 at Ghent in a Jesuit house for aged and infirm missionaries.

The details of his life and literary career are necessarily obscure, especially the period before he went to Rome. A manuscript of 1613 from the English College there speaks of him as 'very learned in the English laws, and that he had left a wife, office, and many other commodities and expectations to become a priest in the Seminaries' (H. Foley, *Records of the English Province of the Society of Jesus*, III, 1878, p. 491). This may mean that he renounced the prospect of marriage and a comfortable life, and that he at one time studied the law, perhaps at the Inns of Court, although no record of this has been discovered. Prior to his first book, *A Survey of the Apostasy of Marcus Antonius de Dominis*, [S. Omer] 1617, a translation of a controversial tract by Father John Floyd, there is only a sonnet signed by H. H., 'To the ternall, and aeternal Vnitie', found in the second edition of Thomas Wright's *The Passions of the Minde*, 1604, which has been tentatively ascribed to him. Wright, a somewhat enigmatical Jesuit who attempted to mediate between English Catholics and the Government (v. T. A. Stroud, 'Father Thomas Wright: a Test Case for Toleration', *Biographical Studies*, 1, 1951), may have known the Hawkins family but the initials H. H. could well be those of the Catholic poet Hugh Holland.

After his early venture into controversial theology, probably undertaken at the request of his superiors, Hawkins only wrote books of devotion and spiritual edification. They show his firm and fervent Catholic faith, a remarkable freedom from narrow sectarianism and an emphasis on the divine love, the consolations of the spiritual life and the beauty and richness of creation, which he turned to meditative use within the framework of a 'symbolical theology', a concept derived from Sandaeus's *Theologia Symbolica* (Lottes, *op. cit.*, p. 67). His books must have been of great help to suppressed English Catholics, harassed by fines and persecutions, cut off from the normal life of their own church, and in danger of cultural and intellectual isolation. The books were smuggled into England after having been printed abroad, at first by the Jesuits at their S. Omer press, then from 1632 by Cousturier at Rouen, who did much of his printing for Recusants. The change to Cousturier was probably due to the financial troubles of the S. Omer press at that time. Hawkins would have done most of his actual writing in England and would only seldom have been able, after a dangerous journey, to attend to publication on the Continent. It appears that he resided mainly in London and the South of England, where most of his friends and relatives lived. He spent some time at the Jesuit residence at Clerkenwell and may have secretly visited the town house of his family in the parish of St. Sepulchre's where his brother Thomas, according to his will, kept 'musicke Bookes'; the 'Violls' were kept at Nash Court (Public Record Office, Prob. 11/185, fol. 41). Music seems to have had a particular attraction for Recusant families (cf. F. M. McKay, 'A Seventeenth-Century Collection of Religious Poetry', *Bodleian Quarterly Record*, 8, 1970, p. 191).

The dedications in some of Hawkins' books give an idea of where he found support and encouragement and, perhaps, an occasional resting place from his labours. 'The Noble and Most Worthy Knight Syr B. B.', whose patronage and bounty are acknowledged in *Fuga Saeculi*, is Sir Basil Brooke, a friend of the family, collaborator with Sir Thomas Hawkins in the translation of *The Holy Court*, and generally prominent in Catholic affairs and at Court, and also concerned, together with Endymion Porter, with the mining of iron ore in the West Midlands (*Calendar of State Papers, Domestic*, May 1638, p. 395). Hawkins' 'Maecenas', Henry Nevill, Lord Abergavenny (v. *The Sweete Thoughts of Death, and Eternity*), and Lady Mary Teynham (v. *The History of S. Elizabeth*) belonged both to his native county of Kent and to that network of related noble Catholic families which included the Ropers, Petres, Sackvilles, and Vauxs of Harrowden. Lady A. W., in *The Life of S. Aldegond*, can be identified as Lady Anne Arundell of Wardour whose full name is given in Miles Car's [Miles Pinkney's] *A Draught of Eternitie* (Allison and Rogers 195). She supported the Church and distressed Catholics, and was patroness of a Marian Sodality in England, perhaps the same for which Hawkins wrote *Partheneia Sacra*. She died in 1637 at Lennox House in Drury Lane, London. Her husband, the first Lord Arundell, was a Count of the Holy Roman Empire and a great benefactor to the Church (v. Joseph Jackson Howard, *Genealogical Collections illustrating the History of Roman Catholic Families in England*, privately printed, n.d., part iii; G. E. C., *Complete Peerage*, 1910, I, p. 263). Of particular interest is the dedication, in 1634, of *The Devout Hart* 'To the R. Worthy and Vertvovs Covple, W. Standford Esq[r], and Elizabeth his wife'. They are not easily identified but appear to belong to the ancient Staffordshire Catholic families of Stan[d]-ford of Packington and Perry Hall, and Comberford of Comberford, all places in or near the present city of Birmingham. The marriage of William Stanford of

Packington, living in 1583, and Elizabeth, daughter of Thomas Comberford (d. 1597), is recorded in a manuscript in the William Salt Library, Stafford (SM 288, p. 83) and in the Staffordshire pedigrees. They would have been about seventy in 1634 and could very well be Hawkins' 'Vertvovs Covple'. He had probably been introduced to them by another Jesuit missionary and author, Robert Stanford (1593–1659) of the Perry Hall branch of the family, who taught at the colleges of S. Omer and Watten and became Rector of the English College, Rome, in 1641 (cf. Allison and Rogers 225 and 285). Two of Robert's brothers also 'went beyond the sea' (v. S. Shaw, *History of Staffordshire*, II, 1801, p. 109). Hawkins' intimate mode of addressing the Stanfords, '*My Dearest*', and his desire to profess himself '*to al the world, to be* Your most obliged and deuoted H. A.', suggests that he knew them well and that he extended his travels and missionary activities as far as the Midlands. The Recusant Rolls and other documents give the impression that here the Catholic gentry suffered more than the noble Catholic families in the South. In 1635, John, the son of William Stanford of Perry Hall, was found with other children in the house of Mr. Leveson being trained as a scholar under a priest or Jesuit and was removed to the house of his grandfather Sir John Persall of Horseley (v. *Calendar of State Papers, Domestic*, 9 December 1635). Could Hawkins have been that 'priest or Jesuit'? Later, in the Civil War, Colonel Edward Stanford, the squire of Perry Hall and a brother of the Jesuit Robert, was sequestered and imprisoned as a Recusant and Royalist (Order Book of the County Committee 1643–45, *Staffordshire Historical Collections*, 1959, p. 240). Such were the people for whom the Jesuits wrote their books as part of their missionary effort. Without the support of these people the books could not have been written, as Robert Stanford acknowledges in his *Nicetas or The Triumph ouer Incontinencie*, 1633, a translation from Drexelius (Allison and Rogers 285): '*To you therefore the ornament of your Country, the high honour of Catholicke Religion (which with hazard of your liues and daylie losse of goods and liberty you so constantly defend) I dedicate this my little booke. To you I present it, rather as an acknowledgement then payment of the debt I owe you*' (sig. ã2^{v}).

In the short dedication of *The Devout Hart* Hawkins alludes to the combined effect of emblem and meditation he wants to achieve. '*I heer present you with a HART, not fram'd of flesh and bloud . . . but liuely deciphered with deuout Embleams: Pictures (as* Symonides *saith) are silent Poesies, and Poesies speaking pictures. Both the one and the other are heer exhibited to your viewes, accompanyed with deuout Meditations, where euery title speakes but the loue of IESVS*' (pp. 3–4). His method is best understood by looking at the sources of the work. The prototype is *Le coeur devot, trone royal de Jesus Pacifique Salomon*, (Paris) 1626, by the French Jesuit Etienne Luzvic, written for a religious community, perhaps one devoted to the Sacred Heart (cf. Luzvic's epistle 'To the Amorovs and Devovt Harts to Iesvs', *Devout Hart*, pp. 7–13). There were no illustrations. An enlarged edition appeared in the following year at Antwerp and Douay: *Le coeur devot, Throsne royal . . . auquel sont promises les sainctes faueurs du petit Iesus au coeur qu'il ayme et qui l'ayme, par le R. P. Etienne Binet.* Father Binet, the Jesuit Provincial for the Champagne, also wrote the lives of St. Aldegond and of St. Elzear, the first of which was to be translated by Henry Hawkins and the second by Sir Thomas Hawkins. Binet's contribution to *Le coeur devot* was based upon his work *Les saintes faveurs du petit Jesus au coeur*, (Paris) 1626, an early example of the cult of the Infant Jesus.

However, the most important addition in the 1627 version of *Le coeur devot* proved to be the twenty emblematic engravings of the heart signed 'Mart. Baes fec.', which Martin Baes or Basse had adapted from the famous series of eighteen pictures with Latin verses, *Cor Iesu amanti sacrum*, created by Anton Wierix at Antwerp about 1600 (v. Mario Praz, *Studies in Seventeenth-Century Imagery*, 2nd. ed., 1964, pp. 152–54, 407, 535; Adolf Spamer, *Das kleine Andachtsbild*, 1930, pp. 151–54; L. J. Alvin, *Catalogue Raisonné de l'Oeuvre des Trois Frères Jean, Jerome et Antoine Wierixe*, (Brussels) 1866). These engravings are of excellent workmanship and were produced either as a series or as single prints, or for the illustration of devotional books, and gained widespread popularity. They depict Christ consecrating the heart, freeing the heart from the world, the flesh, and the devil, knocking at the door of the heart, sweeping the monsters of vices out of the heart, cleaning the heart with expiatory blood, resting in the heart, wounding the heart with the arrows of divine love, celebrating the heavenly nuptials in the heart, and, lastly, manifesting himself and the Holy Trinity in the heart (see the list of emblems at the end of this Note).

There had been isolated examples of religious heart-emblems (v. Georgette de Montenay's *Emblemes ou Devises Chrestiennes*, 1571, Scolar Press, Continental Emblem Books series, No. 15, 1973, pp. 27, 29, 30) but *Cor Iesu amanti sacrum* is the first fully developed series of 'cardiomorphic' emblems. Notable later sequences occur in Daniel Cramer's *Emblemata Sacra*, 1624, Johann Mannich's *Sacra Emblemata LXXVI*, 1625, Benedict van Haeften's *Schola Cordis*, 1629, and the English version of it by Christopher Harvey in 1647, and Francisco Pona's *Cordiomorphoseos sive ex corde desumpta Emblemata sacra*, 1645 (further examples are found in K. A. Wirth, 'Religiöse Herzemblematik', *Das Herz*, priv. publ. by Dr. Karl Thomae GmbH, Biberach an der Riss, 2, 1966). In these books, a small heart undergoes all sorts of manipulations interpreted in a spiritual way, whereas in Wierix the large heart is itself the scene of Christ's actions. The sequence clearly reflects the old mystical ladder of *purgatio*, *illuminatio*, and *unio*, also the growing cult of the Sacred Heart which had been developed in the late Middle Ages, especially by the Carthusians, from images of the wound in Christ's side and the shield of the Five Wounds (for a comparison of pictures in a Carthusian manuscript with some devotional emblems see my 'Arbor, Scala und Fons vitae', *Chaucer und seine Zeit. Symposion für W. F. Schirmer*, ed. A. Esch, (Tübingen) 1968). The simple woodcut of the Jesuit badge on the title-page of *The Devout Hart*, with the monogram IHS, the cross, the three nails, and the four Greek letters for THEOS in the corners, is derived from such representations of a crowned and wounded heart. Although in the Wierix series the devout heart is the human heart, there has always been in religious heart symbolism a tendency towards identification of the heart of man with that of Christ.

By showing Christ as a child-like figure the Wierix plates have some share in the cult of the Infant Jesus. The ground was prepared when Vaenius turned the Cupids of his *Amorum Emblemata*, 1608, with ease and elegance into the child-like figures of Divine Cupid (Christ) and Anima seen in his *Amoris Divini Emblemata*, 1615, thereby establishing the convention which was later so fruitfully exploited by Hugo and Quarles, and which was afterwards firmly remarried to the cardiomorphic tradition by van Haeften. It should, however, be noticed that these emblem writers look at the pictures in a strictly allegorical way and expect their readers to do the same. Normally they do not address Christ as a child but as almighty and loving God. 'Let not the tender Eye checke, to see the allusion to our blessed SAVIOUR figured, in these Types' (Francis Quarles, 'To the Reader', *Emblemes*, 1635). Hawkins seems at times to be carried away by the tenderness of his love and the direct visual impact of the picture: 'Thy little IESVS, the purest ioy and delight of Heauen, raps at the doore . . .' (p. 48). (His Latin source too, uses the diminutive form of address, 'Iesule', which occurs in Baroque religious lyrics.) So much for the pictures which had been secured for the Luzvic–Binet book of 1627. In the same year Father Charles Musart, S.J., published a Latin translation at Douay, *Cor Deo Devotum, Jesu Pacifici Salomonis Thronus Regius*, which became the model for many further editions and translations throughout Europe including Hawkins' English version. Musart added a dedication 'Parthenicis Mariae Sodalium Xenium' which was, however, omitted by Hawkins. Therefore, neither *The Devout Hart* nor, as Rosemary Freeman states (*op. cit.*, p. 178), *Le coeur devot* was written for a Marian society, only Musart's Latin version.

Hawkins replaced Musart's preliminaries by his own dedication to the Stanfords (pp. 3–6), then comes his translation of Luzvic's dedication (pp. 7–13), which is a summary of the emblematic meaning. This is followed by the twenty emblematic and meditative units. Each of these consists of the picture or Icon (or a blank page where this is missing), the Hymne composed by Hawkins, a prose passage called the Incentive by Binet and the Meditation by Luzvic. On the title-page, Hawkins is at pains to give a fair indication of the several writers' contributions to the work, disguising himself under the description of 'a new hand'. The structure of each meditation follows closely the *Spiritual Exercises* of Ignatius of Loyola: the Preamble, the unchanging Preparatory Prayer, *Actiones nostras quaesumus, &c*, one or two Preludes (these being sometimes omitted), three or four Points, and the Colloquy, the whole meditation to be concluded by *Pater noster* and *Ave Maria*. Of the three principal parts of the Ignatian meditation only the Colloquy (with prayers, petitions, and resolutions) is explicitly mentioned; but the *Compositio loci* (with application of the visual sense) is, of course, represented by the emblematic Icon and its description, and the Analysis of the theological meaning occurs mainly in the Points.

Meditation means the consideration, penetration, and acceptance of a spiritual truth through the senses, the mind, and the will. It should be recalled that Ignatius had devised a programme of exercises or meditations for four weeks. It begins with preparation, self-examination, and the realisation of the powers of sin and hell, continued by contemplations of the life of Christ up to His ascension, and on the most important mysteries of the Christian faith. This programme, which had itself been derived in part from the old *Scala mystica*, could easily be adapted to the notion of spiritual ascent embodied in the twenty plates of the Wierix–Baes series which form the emblematic backbone of Hawkins' book. A few years before, the fusion of emblem and meditation had already been most successfully demonstrated by Hermann Hugo's *Pia Desideria*, 1624. A random example may show how well the meditative *Compositio loci* and the emblematic Icon could be combined: in meditating on something invisible like sin, Ignatius recommends that one should create a picture in the imagination and see how one's soul is incarcerated in this corruptible body of death. Hugo follows this precept in emblem 38 (III, 8, in Quarles), which depicts Anima imprisoned in the thorax of a gruesome skeleton. In another very popular book of emblematic meditations, which served as a model for Hugo, the reader is simply advised: 'COMPOSITIO LOCI, vt in imagine' (v. Antoine Sucqvet, S.J., *Via vitae aeternae*, 1620, p. 469).

Hawkins' own verse contributions, the Hymnes, each consist of seven rhymed couplets. Coming after the title, or Lemma, they must be regarded, in terms of the basically threefold division of the emblem (Lemma, Icon, Epigram), as the Epigram, which should be a poem explaining the Icon. Description and explanation are here often indicated by 'Behold . . .' and 'Loe . . .', and the Wierix plates with their wealth of allegorical detail offer abundant opportunity to prove that 'Meditation considereth by peece-meale the obiectes proper to move us' (Francois de Sales, *A Treatise of the Love of God*, trans. Miles Car [Miles Pinkney], 1630, p. 336). The verses usually conclude with an emotional appeal or resolution and thus form a meditation *in nuce*. It will be noticed that the next section, the Incentive, fulfils a similar function in language even more emotional. In fact, in the Latin version this prose section of Binet's had been called *Imaginis expositio*. By adding his new explanatory poems Hawkins caused a certain duplication, but the style of the two sections is sufficiently distinctive to avoid monotony. As it happened, the doubled explanation proved an advantage in those cases where plates could not be provided. The reader can understand such unillustrated 'naked emblems' quite well, but the lack of visual stimulus means also a serious loss of aesthetic and emotional appeal. One can only speculate about the circumstances. The plates were to be printed not on separate leaves but on the same sheets as the letterpress. This was usually done with a rolling press after the printing of the type and before folding into gatherings. At this stage, difficulties, probably of a financial nature, must have arisen. In 1634, perhaps after some delay, it was eventually decided to bind and publish part of the impression without the plates. By 1638 the plates had become available and were used for the remaining sheets, these copies being supplied with the cancel slip for the date. But because of the scarceness of surviving copies we cannot be sure whether all the 1634 copies were issued without plates and each of the 1638 copies with plates. It should be borne in mind that previous writers on *The Devout Hart* were unaware of the existence of a copy with plates and thought that Hawkins had omitted them from his version (cf. Freeman, *op. cit.*, p. 179). In the Eton copy the plates are unsigned. There are similar plates in a German version by Carl Stengel, *Das Gott zugeeignete Hertz,* (Augsburg) 1630, also unsigned.

Rosemary Freeman's assumption that *The Devout Hart* was written before *Partheneia Sacra* (though published later) is probably correct. The theme of the heart as a flourishing garden (emblem 12) seems to have been expanded into the Marian garden of the second book. Here, the throne of the pacifical Solomon or Christ becomes a type of Virgin Mary (*Partheneia Sacra*, p. 76).

Hawkins' verses show the contemporary fashion for mythological and domestic conceits. Sometimes a basic emblematic conceit, like *Cordis purgatio* in No. 7 (p. 96), can easily be unfolded into further conceits after the manner of the *Schola Cordis*:

Thy contrite hart plow'd, harrowd, sown,
May, watered with his heauenly dew,
Spring forth, and fructify anew.

A certain lack of intellectual and emotional intensity is in part due to the descriptive function of these verses within the emblematic framework, but, as in *Partheneia Sacra*, Hawkins' prose is much better, richer, more imaginative, graphic, and lively than his occasional verse. He manages to preserve the individuality of his prose style in spite of the fact that *The Devout Hart* is a translation. He translates freely, and his situation here is not so very different from that in *Partheneia Sacra* where, as Dr. Lottes points out (*op. cit.*, pp. 66–68), he translates large parts from Jacobus de Voragine and Maximilianus Sandaeus. In *The Devout Hart* Hawkins increases the tenderness, fervour, and sensuousness of his original. His language is throughout imbued with the imagery of the Song of Songs, the Spiritual Marriage between Christ and the Soul, the 'religious Petrarchism' of the Baroque.

On the Continent, the Wierix plates, alone or as part of religious books, became immensely popular. They were imitated and adapted for Latin, French, Dutch, German, and Italian publications, some as late as 1883. Nearly all of them were prepared for the use of Catholic readers. I know of only one version clearly written for Protestants: *Himmlisches Freuden-Mahl*, by M. J. Rittmeyer, (Helmstädt) 1703, and later editions, with ten of the Wierix emblems (cf. John Landwehr, *German Emblem Books*, 1972, Nos. 506–9). In Britain, the direct influence of a Recusant publication like *The Devout Hart* was limited. But printsellers or travelling print-collectors like Nicholas Ferrar and Edward Benlowes must have brought the curious, finely-engraved, plates with their Latin verses into the country; they were available in the Netherlands from about 1600. John Wontneel alias Hans Woutenel was such a printseller and agent for Dutch firms. He was active in London up to *ca* 1614 and was reported to the authorities as being an importer of Popish books (A. M. Hind, *Engraving in England*, I, 1952, p. 284; *Historical Manuscripts Commission, Salisbury MSS.*, part x, p. 62).

There is a great deal of religious 'cardiomorphic' imagery to be found in seventeenth-century English poetry. In many instances reference to a pictorial or emblematic 'source' would be futile. Often the verbal and the pictorial image derive from the same biblical metaphor. But sometimes the analogy to a Wierix emblem and its interpretation is so close that the emblem may, at some stage in the development of the image, have exercised a formative influence. In Donne's *Holy Sonnet XIV*, 'Batter my heart, three person'd God', the contrast between God's soft knocking at the door of the heart and his forceful battering of the gates of the heart may have been suggested to the poet by the shadowy recollection of a small picture, Wierix's emblem 3 (cf. my article 'Eine Emblemfolge in Donnes *Holy Sonnet XIV*', *Archiv*, 200, 1963). Emblems 5, 'Jesus sweeps the dvst of Sinnes from the hart', and 7, 'Jesus purgeth the Hart with expiatory blood', seem to be echoed in Herbert's 'Church-floor' and in Bunyan's Interpreter's House; emblem 4, 'Jesus searcheth out the Monsters lurking in the darke corners of the hart', also in Vaughan's 'The Feast'. Roger Sharrock has pointed out the similarity between the Wierix and Bunyan 'emblems' ('Bunyan and the English Emblem Writers', *Review of English Studies*, 21, 1945), but no direct link has been established. Perhaps there were intermediate pictorial sources. *The Soules Soulace; or Thirtie and one Spirituall Emblemes*, 1631, by the printseller Thomas Jenner, symbolizes 'A Remedie against Despaire' (No. 3) by the simple engraving of a man pouring water on the pavement of a '*Hall*, Or other roome'. Quite apart from the question of sources, *The Devout Hart* with its plates provides full examples of how a number of ideas, images, and conceits which are, literally, close to the human heart, could be formed, developed, and interpreted. It shows in rare detail, like a magnifying glass, the interaction of visual and verbal imagination. It is an invaluable record of seventeenth-century sensibility.

KARL JOSEF HÖLTGEN

UNIVERSITY OF
ERLANGEN-NÜRNBERG

A LIST OF THE EMBLEMS IN *THE DEVOUT HART*

M. DC. XXXVIII.

THE DEVOVT HART OR ROYAL THRONE OF THE PACIFICAL Salomon.

Composed by F. St. Luzuic S. I. Translated out of Latin into English.

Enlarged with Incentiues by F. St. Binet of the same S. and now enriched with Hymnes by a new hand.

Printed by Iohn Cousturier.

1634.

TO THE R. WORTHY AND VERTVOVS COVPLE, W. STANDFORD ESQ[r], AND ELIZABETH his wife.

MY DEAREST,

I heer present you with a HART, not fram'd of flesh and bloud, the seat and citadel of the vital spirits, but the image of a HART *fully fraught with pious and amorous affects; a hart, not in idæa, but liuely deciphered with deuout Embleams. Pictures (as* Symonides *saith) are silent Poesies, and Poesies speaking pictures. Both the one and the other are heer exhibited to your viewes, accompanyed with deuout Meditations, where euery title speakes but the loue of* IESVS. *If you eye wel and marke these silent Poesies, giue eare to these speaking pictures, but chiefly make vse of the Meditations in the repose of your recollected thoughts, you wil proue by a happy experience how proper they are to rayse a soule to a soueraigne aspiration of diuine things. The Authours Preface points you forth his scope, and his whole discourse displayes it better; to which I referre you, and my self and labours heerin to your more fauourable acceptation, that could not be satisfyed but with thus expressing and professing my selfe to al the world, to be*

Your most obliged
and deuoted
H. A.

TO THE AMOROVS AND DEVOVT HARTS TO IESVS.

I Present you, my HARTS most deare to Iesus, with a wounded HART, enflamed al with diuine loue. This is the Royal Throne of your Spouse the Pacifical *Salomon*, the Sanctuary wherin God would haue perpetual Sacrifice to be offred, the Tower which IESVS hath taken to defend against al hostile inuaſion ; which being wrongfully vſurped , and ſacrilegiouſly profaned,he recouers, purgeth, expiates, then takes and cōſecrates for his Palace, Temple, and Tribunal. Here *Ieſus* exerciſes his commands, here he raignes , here he teacheth , here cutting off al demurres of appeales he pronounceth ſentence of eternal predeſtination or reprobation ; here he rayſeth thunders and lightnings , here ſweetly dartes he rayes of light, not vſually ſeen in this ſublunary Globe. Finally I offer here the HART, the heauen and Court of the ſupreame Moderatour of ſoules.

But why especially to you? Surely I should thinke this guift could be no-where held in more esteeme or taken for a greater fauour, then by you, whom I know wel to be not only singularly trayned vp and exercised in these diuiner things, but so ardently affected to them, as that you set by the loue of this one *IESVS* more then al the graces and fauours of Kings & Princes in the world: Since in your soules the Crosse of Christ and loue of holy pouerty, is deeper and more strongly imprest, then al those mushrumps of honours, that pelf of riches, those

Grand-Sires ſeales, and famous images of old, then al thoſe goods, ſo commonly called, which men of your ranck and quality either eaſily promiſe to themſelues, or more ambitiouſly hunt after.

I preſent to you a breife Table, wherin (ſpeaking with modeſty) I haue ſuccinctly delineated in short points of meditations the ſumme of al Chriſtian perfection, and that meerly for your ſakes, and the reſt who thinke and loue the ſame with you; where no ſooner shal you fix your eyes on that image of Diuine loue, how il pourtraicted soeuer with a ride pencil, but you shal easily discerne, I trow, a liuely Image, truly represented, of al those faire and goodly vertues you haue formed in your mindes, and shal find no doubt by what wayes and degrees the diuine goodnes hath led you to the top of this Mount, from whence, remayning yet on earth, you may contemplate euen heauen it-self, that land of promise, and blessed inheritance of the children of God; and where you haue the most calamitous regions of the vnfortunate *Aegypt* and *Babylon*, the mother of confusion, not only ſubject to your eyes, but trod vpon and trampled vnder-foot. Accept then, my ſoules moſt deare to heauen, this guift ſuch as it is, not regarding ſo much the hand which giues, as the giuers hart. For my part I haue but dipt, as I may ſay, my finger in the hony-combs, which here lye hid in certayne figures and Images, as folded vp in wax: but the Holy Ghoſt, I truſt, wil copiouſly deriue the pureſt hony thence, and conſequently open the very fountaines of nectar it-ſelf, and moſt aboundantly dew your minds with ſhowers of diuine graces ; ſo doe I hartily vow , ſo wish , remayning,

Your moſt humble and obedient ſeruant in Chriſt.

STEVEN LVZVIC.

IHS
COR
IESV
AMANTI
SACRVM

THE HART
CONSECRATED
to the loue of IESVS.

THE HYMNE.

IESV, behold the hart dilates
  It-selfe to thee, and consecrates
It's triple power, and al within.
  But oh! that heauy burden, sinne,
Drawes to the earth, and makes it fal
  From high aspiring thoughts. Not al,
Who now support, giue it repose;
  Thou art the Atlas, here enclose
Thy selfe within the hart, giue rest
  To it, which otherwise opprest, (down.
With the heauy load, the world, sinks
  Make it despise (to gaine a crowne)
The earth, it's Nathir, and with thee
  It's Zenith make Eternity.

THE

THE INCENTIVE.

1. W*Here our treasure is, there is our hart* (a). IESVS is a treasure, wherin our hopes, our riches, and al we haue, are lodged & laid vp in store. Where then shal we better place the hart, then in the hart, the Reliquary of the diuinity it-self, at IESVS feet, the most sure Altar of the miserable, in his hands, the richest Magazin of al graces?

2. Loe here a hart burning al with loue, how many and what flames it sends forth like a furnace. Happy & thrice happy he, who, but for Heauen, hath no loue, no hart at al!

3. Goe to, then, al you pious and sincere harts, come and consecrate your selues to the honour and loue of IESVS. For to whom better? since what we pay to him we allow

our ſelues; and what we take from him we quite forgoe and looſe for euer.

(a) *Luc* 12.

THE PREAMBLE TO THE firſt Meditation.

W*Ho ſhal ſeuer vs from the charity of Chriſt?* (exclaymes that great Apoſtle) *tribulation? or diſtreſſe? or famine? or nakedneſſe? peril? perſecution? or the ſword? Sure I am, that death, nor life, nor Angels, nor Principates, nor vertues, nor preſent, nor future things, nor fortitude, altitude, nor depth, nor any other creature, can ſeperate vs from the charity of God, which is in Chriſt* IESVS (a). This is the fire, which gliding from heauen conſumes al things, burnes al things; yea enkindles ſuch flames as euen the Ocean of euils, wherewith the world flowes,& aboundes,cã not quench-it. This ſubtil, actiue, ſpreading, and deuouring flame, takes force & vigour euen from very croſſes and torments themſelues, ſurmounts al things,cleaues to one God;and with an inextricable knot is vnited with him. Whether it be the fire, which alwayes ſuffers ſome-what,or actuates this or that,I know not;this I am ſure of, that the liuelyer it puts forth the force it hath,the leſſe it yealds to the enemy, and is the hardiyer ouercome. This fire,when once it takes on the litle furnace of the hart, good God! what ſtrange, and how many heates, of loue enkindles it there? They only know the exceſſes of this vnquiet feauer, who loue IESVS deerely indeed,& paſſionately thirſt after him.

Now ſhal you ſee this languiſhing hart breake out into frequent, ab-

rupt,

rupt, and interrupting ſighs, and now and then heare certayne brieſe interiections withal, caſt forth here and there by the poore ſoule, liquefying with a ſweet extaſy of loue: *Tel my beloued*, o bleſſed ſpirits, *that I languish al for loue* (b) and that vnles with the prop of his golden ſcepter he come, as once *Aſſuerus* to *Heſter* (c) & powerfully ſuſteyne & hold vp my fleeting ſoule, I ſhal faint at his feet: for now the vnequal and feeble pulſe euen mortally beates, and now my face is fouly dight with an asky and deadly colour, the extatical heat now wholy waſtes the marrow, ſo as now remaynes in me nothing which ſuffers not of this fire.

But anon you wil wonder to ſee that hart excited with the ſame loue of God, reſuming as it were new ſtrength, to be ſodainly caryed and

ſnacht

ſnacht with violence into the thing beloued. *I wil riſe*, ſaid the Spouſe extreamly enamoured with her beloued, *I wil compaſſe the Citty, through ſtreets and lanes, I wil ſeeke whom my ſoule loues* (d); nor wil I giue ouer til obteyning my deſire I take hold of him. I wil enquire of created things, & aske them, where is my God? I wil ſeeke and perticularly demand of al; nor wil I truely reſt ſatisfyed finding ſome image only of God in them ſuperficially ſhadowed, or diſcouering but a glimmer only of diuine perfections, for theſe wil but excite my thirſt, not quenh it wholy; but I wil hunt further and conſtantly ſeeke him, *whom my ſoules loues* (e). For the hart enflamed with loue, continually machinates & workes ſomething; nor hath diuine loue learned to be idle: it is alwayes in action, and ſtil proceedes from vertue to

vertue,

vertue, and if it rest at any tyme, and seeme but to sabothize, it is no longer diuine loue (f).

Amidst these symptomes of this disease, the mind obteynes three things, and proues them in it-selfe: for first, how much soeuer it occupyes it-self in difficult things, and seriously attends, to its owne abasement, to a perfect contēpt of worldly things, to represse vntamed and vnbridled appetites, yet al these acts, most worthy and heroical, it puts in the last place, yea when it workes and effects the most, thinks it hath done as good as nothing, and lastly accounts the tyme so long spent in the lists of vertue to be exceeding short, which euen the sacred Scriptures record of the Patriarch *Iacob*, whom the beauty and loue of the faire *Rachel* had so taken & enveigled, as he reckoned yeares very tedious for toyles, as weekes for dayes, dayes for moments(*g*). I haue yet said but litle: The hart which is enamoured with IESVS, thinks it cannot be broken or tamed with any thing, and therefore dares prouoke euen death it-self, & chalenge it to a single fight, as not his match, to scorne its weapons, and not so only, but insolently to insult vpon this pale Goddesse, who yet is she which tramples the Crownes and Scepters of Kings and *Cæsars*, subdues the armed *Sampsons* and layes them at her foot, forbids the *Alexanders*, not satisfyed with one world, to spread their Ensignes any further; lastly, puts the *Helenaes*, as deformed, vnder a base yoke. What more? This hart is so impatient of rest, delayes, al things, as while most ardently it loues and seekes the onelie IESVS, and groanes after him, it holds a mo-

ment

ment for a yeare , regards not any thing els , nothing likes , nothing pleaſeth , nothing ſatiates or recreates a whit, as to whom, beſides IESVS, al things are nauſeous and but dreames vnto it. Laſtly, for his ſake, after whom it ſighes and languiſhes with the heat of thirſting loue, ſcorning the ſtinking lakes of wordly pleaſures, and the filthy mire of the *Ægyptian* bogs, like a Stag nigh periſhing with thirſt and deadly wounds , with a rapid courſe and willing mind , ruſhes through the brakes and craggy rocks of precipices, and haſtes to the founteynes of endles waters , *to God the liuing ſpring* (h).

Oh inexhauſtible ſpring of loue , quench this thirſt , ſatiate this hunger ! *O beauty ſo antient* (i) *and ſo yong*! take here poſſeſſion of the hart deuoted to thee. Be this I pray a

Temple,

Temple, a Chapel, an Altar conſe-crated to the true and only Godhead. Admit the incenſe (k) in an odour of ſweetnes, which ſhal hereafter fume from this golden table, nor euer ſuffer, o God of my hart, the place thus duly dedicated to thy honour and loue, to be euer once defiled with ſorditryes or crimes, but rather may it euer and euer ſtand inuiolable and vntouched.

(a) *Rom.* 8. (b) *Cant.* 5. (c) *Eſter* 15. (d) *Cant.* 3. (e) *Cant.* 1. (f) *Greg. Hom.* 30. *in Euang.* (g) *Gen.* 29. (h) *Pſal.* 41. (i) *Auguſt. Conſ. lib.* 10. *cap.* 21. (k) *Exod.* 37. & 40.

I. MEDITATION.

I. MEDITATION.

The Preparatory Prayer.

Actiones nostras quæsumus, &c.

First Prelude.

IMagin God being in Heauen, seated on the *Cherubins*, most highly blessed, and in essential perfection infinit, to require here on earth an Inne to lodge in.

2. Prelude.

Imagin the Tabernacle erected of old, through diuine precept, by *Moyses* (a) there the Temple by *Salomon* (b) most sumpteously and magnificently built, and therein the Propitiatory reposed whence diuine Oracles were afforded to men.

The hart of a pious man &.a Temple of the Godhead, and hath

three parth with it, whereof the firſt the mind, is to be ſeen in the vpper place. Here God in the production of things, as in a high Altar, propoſeth the omnipotency to be ſeen and worſhiped in the gouern'ment of them the higheſt wiſdome, and the infinit goodnes in the conſeruation. The interiour part of the Temple is the other portion of the hart, the wil; and here that infinit either goodnes, or beauty aboue al things, exhibits it-ſelf moſt amiable. Laſtly for the out moſt face of the whole Temple ſtand the exteriour ſenſes which, as reaſon, & true piety would, religiouſly obey the wil commanding duly diuine things.

2. *Point*. Moreouer, the Conſecration of this Tēple, the hart I meane deuoted vnto God, is performed with the ſame ceremonies, our Temples rightly dedicated are. The manner

of

of ſanctifying Temples is, to ſtrew the pauements al with aſhes; to affige twelue Croſſes on the wal; to burne as many tapers ſet before them, to haue water bleſſed after the ſolemne formulary of Proceſſions, and in the Aſhes ſprinckled on the ground, the Greeke & Latine Alphabet ſcored out. So his hart that would be the Oratory of the God-head, ſhould firſt be imbued with humility and the knowledge of his owne nothing; be illuſtrated with excellent faith, ſigned with the loue of the Croſſe and mortification, as wel inward as outward, be inſtructed by the *Holy Ghoſt*; and laſtly, in like manner, purely, and holily to be cleanſed, with the heauenly waters of diuine graces.

3. *Point* Now then the hart thus dedicated, with ſo many, and ſo chaſt ceremonies, is ſo in the power and

worſhip of the diuinity, as hereafter without a great ſacriledge, and a hainous crime, it may not be violated; & therefore thence forth, by no meanes, ſhould euer any ſordityes be ſeen there, or, as things prophane, the idoles (c) of worldly fantaſies, be there ſuffred to haue admittance.

4. *Point.* The Oratory of the hart ſhould rather be dreſſed & adorned with the worthy tapiſtries of vertues and heauenly ornaments; and great care be had, that neither by night nor day the incenſe of prayer, the fire of diuine loue (d) the gold (e) of charity be wanting, or frequent vowes, prayers; holocauſts, or the reſt of victimes euer faile.

(a) *Exod.* 26. (b) 3. *Reg.* 6. (c) *Ezech.* 8. (d) *Leuit.* 6. (e) *Apoc.* 3.

THE COLLOQVY.

ARe we then to thinke that God truly inhabits on the earth? Since if Heauen, and the Heauens of Heauens be not able no conteyne thee, how much less, this house? (a) What? My deare then (O loue!) it's euen thy place, thy Temple, thy ſeat, thy Tribunal? My IESVS the delight of my ſoule, grãt this day I beſeech thee, thy diuine preſence may conſecrate my hart to thee, as I truely, freely, and voluntarily vow, giue, and dedicate the ſame to thy Maieſty. Poſſeſſe it with the beſt right and aſſure it with ſo firme a tye, as I may not recouer it againe by any law or tyme ſurely I wil not; but from this Propitiatory, begin thou to giue Anſweres; yea ſend downe from heauen, the fire of the Holy Ghoſt, now preſently to conſume the hoaſts, and holocauſts laid on thy Altar. (a) 3. *Reg.* 8. (b) *Reg.* 18. Pater. Aue.

Fallax mundus ornat vultus. Hoc vitare si vis rete
Dolus latet sed occultus Cito Christi sinus pete
Ne crede blanditys. Procul ab insidiys.

2

THE VVORLD, THE FLESH, THE DIVEL, aſſaile the hart, IESVS ſaues it for himſelf.

THE HYMNE.

MYne eyes are open now I ſee
The nets & ſnares prepare for me
The world, and fleſh haue laid their baits
T'allure my hart, the divel waits.
Vvhile pleaſures of a moment [paſt
E're th'are enioyd] entice: He *laſt*
But firſt protectour, midſt thoſe ginnes,
Midſt ſnares, & tangling nets of ſinnes
Lies lurking: And when he'ſpies
The bird enſnared, out he flies:
O IESV, may my prayer be heard,
Spread forth thy nets, I am thy bird
To catch my hart, 'a Pitfal make
Set lime-twigs, doe but touch & take.

THE INCENTIVE.

1. THe world, with ſilke & golden chaines, the diuel, with horrid and crooked irons, the fleſh with libidinous flames of Hel, through force, through craft, through induſtry, here openly, and here couertly labour very buſily to enſnare, and entrap man's hart. Vnleſſe, good IESV, thou as from an ambuſh doſt ſpeedily reskue it, with thy ſuccours, it is loſt, it is vndone.

2. Looke, what the world ſets forth to ſale are al laid open, but the wines ſhe carouſeth in her golden cup lye hid the brimms are al beſmeared with honny, the gal with in is it, that hurts, that kils. Happy he who by diuine power can wel acquit himſelf of theſe ſnares, theſe nets.

3. And now behold how amourously good IESVS. loues, embraceth, puls this hart vnto himself, and hugs and clings it to his hart. Doe so good IESV; place my hart in thy Heauen; I say, with thy delights and loue, fil, and ouerflow it.

THE PREAMBLE to the Meditation.

HElp here, O Lord of Saboth! Loe bring thy succours hither. The enemies invade thy Sanctuary to pollute the same; they seeke the sacred fires to extinguish them; they violate the Altar of Holocauste to ouerthrow it; they bring in strange and foraine incense, sacrilegiously to burne to their Numens (a) Send downe thy auxiliary bands from heauen; the confederate host of Angels, those spirits, which weild and brandiſh thine armes; els certainly al things wil demoliſh and vtterly periſh: Traynes are ſet on euery ſide, nette and ſnares laid euery-where. God gingerly and take heed if you be wiſe. Here the world that cheating and perfidious Mounte-banck ſete forth his wares, to ſals, precious indeed and ſpecious to the eye at firſt, but whem you heed them bitter, alas meer trumpery and counterfeit ſtuff. The purſe this pedlery merchant ſhewes you, beleeue me, is puffed vp with wind rather then filled with coyne. The diadems glittering al of gold, or rather glaſſe, amid the few and baſtard gemm's, affright with thornes and briars. The cheynes of gold or iewels take which you wil, like iron fetters, honour not, but onerate, and ſtraightly bind. What apparel? The Silk-wormes excrements, with vs being rare,

&

and scarce, are therefore deare; for with the *Thracians* long a goe, these silks haue been but little worth; nor wil they like vs, if not wrought; or interwouen with gold and glitter here and there, with sparckling gemmes. But to what end? forsooth to shroud our nakednes and deformity with a precious mantle. With these allurements then the world seekes to intice to it the hart, and to that end promises huge mountaynes of gold, but yet performes besides the blasts and fickle winds of words, euen iust nothing. For what law can he keep or true fidelity, that wants them both? It is much for it to afford one a vulgar fame, to puffe an empty breath of a little glory which by and by scarce sensible, it blowes another way. For as often as you purchase the grace, not of the vulgar only, but euen of Princes also

with

with the leaſt offence it is ſuddainly ſnatched away from you and leaues you gaping after it, with a light ſmatch only.

Help, help againe O Heauen! Behold here a new enemy at hand the Stygian Dragon, as anciently as ſubtlily trayned vp in this field, that Serpent I meane now ſo long ſince caſt downe to hel (b) from Heauen and that degree of dignity he aymed and aſpired to. The Deuil, I ſay, that Calumniatour, aſſayes to ruſh into thy hold, and that he may hauock and diſturb al things rangeth vp and downe like a fel Lyon in a horrible mãner, that with his dreadful roaring if he cruſh not the hart altogeather, at leaſt he may ſhake it ſhrewdly. Imagine him an Aſpike, his throat to ſwel with poyſon his tooth already faſtened in the wound, the very venome now ready to to come forth, where the ſoule is as good as dead already. Conceiue him a Baſiliske: this as king of ſerpẽts, is more pernitious then the reſt, as he, which with the only eyes inſpireth death, like a theif enchãts the eares with a falſe whiſtle and gently diſtils into the hart a peſt with al: When being gotten in ſoaking the humour thence he pines it vp, and kils it quite? Or ſhal I cal him a Crocadille? You haue then a ſworne enemy no leſſe of our ſaluation then of the heauẽly Court, for he faines our human teares, puts on our effects to deceiue the better. Nor doth *Proteus* ſo transforme himſelf into euery figure, as this pragmatike of the world turnes and winds himſelf euery way into each ſlight. Nor doth this warriour vſe alwayes the ſame weapons or manner of fight for now he takes proſperity for armes, and

now

now aduerſity ; nor leaues he any tyme or place for truce or reſpite. Help therefore, ô you Citizens of heauen, help I ſay! In this combat the *Anthonyes*, the *Hilarions*, and the reſt of Moncks, moſt ſtout Champions, tremble, ſweat, and chaunge ther colour; who ſurely were not ignorant of the forces of this Aduerſary. Is the Casket of the hart repleat with celeſtial riches ? with pride and preſumption of mind he breakes it open, ſteales the treaſure. Is the hart emptie and void of the riches of vertues and the ornaments of diuine graces? with deſpair he attempts to perpetrate any horrible fact; and alwayes bends the artyllery on that ſide he notes to be weaker then the reſt, where he batters ſore and ſhakes the wal, while happily the ſoule attends the leſſe or makes the leſſe reſiſtance. And

holdſt

holdst thou thy peace yet, ô God of Hosts? nor sendst thou as yet, thy subsidiary spirits, with *Michael* their inuincible Captain, to appose a new and stand against this Pest, to chace, pursue, to put to flight, and then so bound to cast it into the inmost dungeon of Hel, where being once shut vp, there may appeare no way for it, to issue forth?

Ay me poore wretch! the external forth thus foyled, the enemy begins to rage at home, the flesh rebels and proud for the good successe of the noble victoryes got vpon those stout aduersaryes of hers, tossеth the warlike fire-brands of concupiscence, here the fires are more dreadful farre then were the Grecians flames. Water, water, I cal for? Rayn down from Heauẽ whole clouds of graces, O the only prop, and stay of my hart, my God; quēch

with

with diuine ſhowers , thoſe fiery weapons , fordged with the helliſh coales; (c) wherewith this impudent brat of *Vulcan*, *Venus* wicked imp , laſciuiouſly armed dares to aſſalt this hart ; which thou thy ſelf wouldeſt haue for Palace, Tower, and Temple.

(a) *Leuit.*10. (b) *Iſaye.*14. (c) *Epheſ.* 6.

II. MEDITATION.

The Preparatory Prayer.

Actiones noſtras. &c.

FIRST POINT.

I Wil conſider the largenes & amplenes of my hart which nothing can fil , neither the vaſtnes of the Heauens , the circuit of the earth, nor Angels , nor men , nor yet riches or delights , themſelues and that

that but he only is able to fil and bleſſe it, who framed it for himſelf.

2. *Point.* Hence wil I gather the worthines and noblenes of my hart, while it contemnes al created things nor vſeth them otherwiſe then as a foot-ſtoole or ſtayers, by ſetting foot, where on it, may mount to God himſelf. So from the odour and beauty of flowers, aſcends it to the ſweetnes and glory of the Creatour, from the light of the San-climbs it to the light increated, from the framing of the world, it findes out the influence of diuine loue into other things, and diſcouers therein a certain plenty and affluence of his guifts.

3. *Point.* I wil further weigh how great muſt the beauty of mans hart be, with whoſe loue al things are ſo enamoured, as vehemently to wiſh

to

haue ſome place, in the ſecret cabinet thereof. The world, that woes it with alluremẽts of honours, riches, iewels, and with the ſame guile the fleſh in preſenting enticemẽts, pleaſures, feaſts, banquets, good fellowſhips, playes, reuels, ſinging and enchanting bewitches it wholy: The diuel, being pleaſed better to vſe violence, ſeekes rather with engins, and frightful terrours to addreſſe his way. Now theſe three enemyes al conſpire in one, and to worke more effectually their ends with a wicked treaſon of the fiue ſenſes, by vndermining ſeeke to ſurpriſe it. To the eyes they ſtreight obiect what ſoeuer is pleaſant & beautiful to behold; whether you would the delicious ſnes of flowers, or rather regard the luſtre of Adamants & the reſt of ſtones. To the eares, they apply their melodious ditties, both perilous

& lasciuious songs of *Syrens* Odours & sweet perfumes are couveighed to the nostrils with ful sayles. For the palat the kitchings fume, daintyes are dressed, and serued vp in ful dishes; wines are fetched from Cellars, tẽpered for the anciens Cõsuls, *Albana Tiuoly* , *Romanesco* , *Falerna*, and the like. And so likewise for the other senses delights are studiously sought for with al industry and art.

4. *Point*. IESVS on the contrary, togeather with the *Angel Gardian*, very seriously defendes the Tower of the hart; he there succours it with the singular assistãce of his diuine grace, this here , in pouring forth light amid the thicke obscureties therein, teacheth what to shun and what it is be done breakes the engins laid against it, repels the assaults of the world, detects the obscenes of the flesh.

THE COLLOQVY.

O MOST ſweet IESV the loue of my hart which thou haſt conſecrated for thy ſelf: Oh permit not in the wals of this Temple the abhominable figures of created things to be ſeen : barricado thy Tower beſeiged of al ſides by enemyes (a) with the countermure of thy feare, defend it with the flames of loue. Thou eaſily deteceſt how falſe the things are which the world obiects before our eyes, while here the miſerable hart diſcernes nor heeds the nets nor poiſon. Then help it I beſeech thee, O Lord of Saboth, in theſe ſtreights, and ſend thy warlike ſquadrons, down from heauen, to its ayd.

(a) *Ezech.* 8,

Pater, Aue.

Vltro cordis portā pultat
IESVS ſilet, et auſcultat
Vocem ſui corculi.

Cor exſurge vectem ſolue
Quid ſit opus factu, volue
In aduentum Sponſuli

3.

THE MOST AMOVROVS IESVS KNOCKS AT the doore of the hart.

The Hymne.

I Saw a little glimps of light
As I lay slumbring in the night,
Vvhich through a cranny of my wal
Glaunc'd on mine eyes, & there-with-al,
I heard one speake, and rapping hard,
Vvhile al my doores were lockt & bar'd
Vvith that I half awakt lookt round,
And in my hart a theife I found
Discouered by the light. The wals
Vvere bare, & naked, while he cals
Vvho stood without, more light appeares,
T'augment my hopes, & lessen feares;
Then, IESV, I cry'd out, come in,
Here's nought but a priuation sinne.

THE INCENTIVE.

1. HOw often hath IESVS, to enter into the Tower of thy hart, assayied it with armes, to wit, with the engines of loue, that to the Angels thou mighst I be a Paradise, to him a Heauen; if thou let him in. O iron hart? O hart of Adamant? God stil is knocking at thy Gates, and is not yet admitted in.

2. But how great is the fauour of this louing Numen? God, euen God himselfe attendes thee, pryes, and lookes about him, watching tyme and place to enter in, that he might sweetly rest with thee. But thou sticktst vpon it, while the Angelical spirits stand amazd thereat, as I may say, either at this goodnes of God, or thy pertinacity, yet thou art nothing mooued.

3. Oh

3. Oh vngrateful hart! oh perfidiousnes! To whom wilt thou yeald them, if to so patient and sweete a louer peeuishly thou holdst out longer. If thou flyest as coylie as constantly he sues?

THE PREAMBLE to the Meditation.

O Fayrest soule among the faire, awake; for what Lethean sleep oppresseth thee? Thy little IESVS, the purest ioy and delight of Heauen, raps at the doore: the golden locks of his head are wet yea trickle with the nightly dewes; his fingers stil the primest mirrh; (a) he wholy drowned and melt with al beates at the gate of thy hart. Open then and let him in Alas how thy doores are frozen with the rock of *Caucasus*! How soundly thou sleepest, oh slug,

O foolish soule! Or is it the noyse perhaps of the Ghests thou hast admitted in already, which so taked vp, and stupifies thine eares, as thou canst not heare thy beloued's voyce? Oh Ghests, or hanting Ghosts I may cal you rather! Oh sinister affections! Oh inordinate appetits! What a tumult haue you made here? And thou, a stony hart! How long hast thou been so hard to heare, and deafe, as not to aduert the Spouses voyce, who to blesse & enrich thee, meerly pushed, with what winde of beatitude I know not, hath touch'd on this vnfaithful Port? Alas! stay I beseech thee, stay a-while, most radiant Sunne, nor with thy swifter steedes, make hast away; for if thou once subtractst thy self, I feare thou wilt goe farre enough, and be long absent: a fauour freely offred once, and lost by a repulse, is not easily recouered. The diuine hand powrs out it's benefits for a day, an hower, a moment only, it lists not alwayes to attend to worke miracles, or to be curing maladyes: the Angel moues the water of that Poole, (b] but on a certaine time of the day; if thou suffrest occasion once to slide away, or be taken by another, thou art to attend the returne of another Angel-mouer. Hasten therefore, O fayrest of al beautyes; what? sleepst thou yet? shake off this sluggishnes. Is there a mutiny at home then quiet the tumults, commaund silence, bid the doore be set open. And if thy Spouse now wearied with thy demurrs should chance to diuert from thee, and goe his wayes, follow him at the heeles with cryes, & prayers, and tyring him out-right, vrge him hard, that he would deyne to returne againe to his Sanctuary. If yet being

being called vpon he goe fly'ng ſtil away. *Like a she-Goat or nimble pricket on the mountaines of Bethel*: (c) double thy cryes, put out thy throat, & cry aloud, *Draw me after thee and we shal ruun* (d) my beloued. If the watchmen of the wals lay hold on thee, and beat thee cruelly, yea, take away thy cloke from thee: let al theſe miſchiefs moue thee nothing; the prey thou huntſt for with al theſe ſame, is cheap enough. Sigh therefore and groane the while, and priuily ſhoot forth the fiery ſhafts of vehement loue; and if thou canſt, wound him flying with the alluring treſſes (e) of thy deſires, with which chaines at leaſt, ſo thrown vpon him, ſtay his flight: and when thou art ſo happy as to ouertake him, now grown at length more ſlack, through flight, thy wound, and chaines ſo hampering him, pray entreat, and beſeech him, by the holy Wounds of his body; *For his ancient and faithful mercies ſake*, (f) he would pleaſe to permit himſelf to be led back againe to his Spouſes houſe. But ſee you hold him faſt (g) nor let him goe; he is a lightning, and paſſeth in an inſtant; he is a Sunne whoſe reuolution is without reſt, nor euer ſtops but at the voyce of the true *Ioſue*, and the couragious ſoule, fighting valiantly againſt the Gabaonites. (h)

This *Sampſon* (h) carryes the gates of the Citty with him, when he feeles himſelf but tampered in the enemyes ſnares, bind him, if you catch him; tye him faſt, with the triple cord of loue, for this *is hardly broken* (k) Laſtlye if now being caught he try, as once the Angel did with *Iacob*, by wraſling to ſtrugle and eſcape away, tel him roundly, *I wil not let thee goe til thou giuest me thy bleßing* (l) But hola thou happyest of soules thou doue, thou darling, take heed thou sufferest not thy self to be ouer-seen so any more; but as soone as thy beloued's voyce shal sound the word that I E S V S comes, boldly and confidently open both the leaues of thy hart vnto him, receiue him; hug him in thy armes, in thy besome, in thy bowels with thy whole hart. (a) *Cant.* 5. (6) *Probatica, Ioan.* 5. (c) *Cant.* 2. (d) *Cant.* 4. (e) *Cant.* 4. (f) *Psal.* 88. *Isaiæ* 55. (g) *Cant.* 3. (h) *Iosue.* 10. (i) *Iud.* 16. (k) *Eccl.* (l) *Gen.* 3.

III. MEDI.

III. MEDITATION.

The Preparatory Prayer.

Actiones nostras quæsumus, &c.

FIRST POINT.

THE louer IESVS, after a weary ſearch in vayne, of a quiet place to reſt in, hauing ſpent therein a long and tedious night a broad with his head euen hoary with the ſerene and nightly dewes (a) knockes at the gate of thy hart, (b) and becauſe thou lockſt him out; greeues and complains againſt thee.

2. *Point.* I wil ſeeke out the cauſe of theſe ſo tedious and irkſome delayes, or what is it that ſtope ſo our eares, that we cannot perceiue the ſound & voyce of him that raps at the doore. Surely it is, becauſe the inordi-

inordinate paſſions doe mutiny and tumultuate with in vs, and ſtirre vp, not one only, but many deafe and diſmal tempeſts, now of anger, now puſilanimity, now ſelf loue, and many others; iuſt as it happens in a wel-frequēted Tauerne, where the Gheſts make ſuch a noyſe among themſelues, as one cannot heare another, that one knowes not who comes in or who goes forth, or who knocks at the gate; ſuch a world there is of Gheſts within, ſuch a rabble of al ſorts.

3. *Point.* I wil weigh the danger, leaſt IESVS ſuffering a repulſe, ſo auerted, turne a ſide into ſome by-wayes and corners, ſo as after he may not be found with the miſerable Spouſe any more; whoſe complaints are read in the Canticles (c) in this manner. *I wil ſeeke whom my loues ſoule, in the ſtreets & lanes,* ſaying,

Haue you seen whom my soule loues? The watchmen of the Citty, haue met with me, smit me, and wounded me. (d) Which hurts, wounds, and teares, surely had not been if she had but presently set open her doores to her beloued. (a) *Cant.* 5. (b) *Apoc.* 3. [c] *Cant.* 3. [d] *Cant.* 5.

THE COLLOQVY.

SHAL be framed much after the manner of the earnest instance made heretofore, by the two Disciples going to *Emaus* (a) saying: *Mane nobiscum Domine.* Come into the secret Closet of my hart; for if thou once but turnest thy back, who can follow thee, or euer looke to ouertake thee, that Giant, who in a moment runst from Heauen to earth, like a lightning and thunder-bolt in an instant casts forth a flash

flash, and vanishest with al; and if thou getst not a place to harbour with vs, like a nimble kid or faune, thou takest thy flight to the mountaynes of Bethel, (b) to the heauenly Quyers of blessed spirits. I know somtimes, the stormes of my inordinate concupiscences arising make such obstreperous noyse with in me, as the pulses sound without cannot be heard; but yet doe thou good IESV, through thy power, wherewith thou art able to doe al things breake the brazen barres of the gate, trust back the iron bolts, and so the doores vnlockt, enter into thy house and Sanctuary.

(a) *Luc.* 24. [b) *Cant.* 2.

Pater. Aue.

Dum ſcrutaris in lucernis
Et veſtigas cum laternis
Cor peccatis obſitum,

O quot monſtra deprehendis
IESV, ſcopas in prehendis
Manet culpis perditum

4

IESVS SEARCHETH OVT THE MONSTERS lurking in the darke corners of the hart.

THE HYMNE.

MY sinnes I thought lay out of sight,
But now I see, al comes to light,
When he to search doth once begin,
Who finds an Attome of a sinne
See there an ougly monster breaths,
An other here, with horrid wreathts,
Is lurking in this darksome caue.
Oh had I sooner what I haue
Of light; I think no loathsome beast
Had in my hart, made-vp his nest.
Oh IESV, stil thy beames display,
Al this is but the breake of day.
Vouchsafe to send with lustre heat,
To make it lightsome, feruent, neat.

THE INCENTIVE.

1. SO long as IESVS is absent from my hart. Ah me! what monsters? what sordityes? what *Gorgons*? what wicked fiends? what hels are centered there?

2. When IESVS enters into the hart, and therein pours his light, Good God? what foule, what horrible prodigies of vices the mind discouers there which the eyes had neuer yet detected? I say while IESVS puts forth his rayes, what bestial manners? what perfidiousnes? what blots of an vngrateful mind? what haynous crimes are represented in this detestable hart?

3. At these portents the very Angels tremble. Yet goe thou on, my most sweet IESVS; Illuminate the darksom corners of the soule, cleanse this

this foule infamous ſtable. Amid this *Cymerian* darknes, with glimps of thy light bewray me to my ſelf that being hateful to my ſelf, I may abhorre and ſhune my ſelf and ſo at length may fly to thee, loue nothing els but thee. Oh the only Darling of my ſoule! O only loue of my hart, my little IESVS!

THE PREAMBLE to the Meditation.

LOrd enter then into the Tower ſet open to thee, and diſmantled wholy; which thou long ſince haſt purchaſed with the price of thy bloud, and in this thy triumphal entry, as it were, ſo ſhoot forth the diuine rayes of thy countenance, that the clouds being vaniſhed quite and ſlunck away, the ſtrange portents of vices, and reſtles Enemyes, which

which lurke therein, may be constrayned to fly away. Search Lord with thee shinĩg lamp of thy knowledge al the hidden corners of this thy Sanctuary. Ay-me! what horrible beasts haue we here? What harpyes, what hydreas, or other monsters, more foule and virulent then these, harbour in this Porch of Hel? Ambition auarice, those base and detestable beasts, here set vp their rests here the ominous screechoules, here the black and fatal progeny of rauens, haue built their nest. Oh! my Dearly beloued, goe on; *Search with thy lanterne* (a) the closest corners of the hart, and discouering the swarine of lewd concupiscences, which here euen pester the miserable hart, crush & destroy them quite. I haue groan'd to thee long, but hitherto my sighs were intercepted, and the broken sound of of my ſtrayn'd voyce, the ſtronger out-cryes of the Enemyes, haue ſo choaked and ſtifled, as we could not be heard. Aboue al things (for hence muſt you begin) ſurvey, and illumine, my God, the abſtruſe and winding corners of my mind; and bringing in the light of the knowledge baniſh thence foule ignorāce of things euen neceſſary for the conſeruation of thy Sanctuary. Alas what a faint and languiſhing light of faith haue we here? vnles it borrow force of thy light, it cannot diſſipate the fogs, nigh palpable, which here haue place: whereas if thou ſhal but ſhead the lighteſt beame of thy preſence thereinto, ſtreight ſhal infidelity, apoſtaſy, ignorance of thy myſteries, or any other errour blinding the mind, euen baniſh quite.

Goe forward then, bring thou

thy

thy clearest lamp, into the inmost cabins of my wil. Alas! how foule it is? How like it is *Augias* stable, or a sty for Swine? I blush thereat. How crooked and vntoward is my wil from thine, my God, who are euen rectitude, sanctity and goodnes it-self? Correct, direct this crookednes of mine; frame my vowes and effects to the most iust square and norme of thy diuine wil. But now bring that both of thine into the regions of the memory. Ayme! what corners and windings haue we here againe, of brawles, of enmityes, which frequent thoughts of iniuries feede, foster, & cherish, whereas indeed they should not once be thought vpon. But as soone as thou shalt shine therein I know wel those foule notes of ingratitude, vnmindfulnes of benefits; memory of iniuries, deeply rooted, shal

ſhal cleane be expunged thence:Goe further now if you pleaſe,into thoſe blind holes, ſearch there with in thoſe blacke and vgly dens; I ſay thoſe ſecret allyes of the hart and bowels. Oh how I tremble-at it, to ſee how many ſnakes there are! What ſpiders, what ſcorpions, and other ſuch like plagues, and alas! what a huge ſwarme there is of them? How many buſy buzzing gnats; peeuish waſps, il-fauoured butterflyes! What a vaſt throng of wormes there is, and what a ſtench from thence exhales to heauen-wards!

O thou moſt burning Sunne, who with darting of thy rayes heretofore, didſt ſodainly ſcortch and wither the greene and flourishing Iuy, (b) ſoake and dry vp the noxious humour of concupiſcence, which enuirons the hart, til thou haſt

hast quite exhausted al. The cloudy Pillar (c) in times past, detecting a farre oft, the snares of the Enemy, as a faithful Guide of the way, went before and conducted the people: So let thy heauenly rayes of thy countenance (strike then with a dread and horrour, who haue the face, or rather are so impudent, as to dare once hostily to inuade the hart by thee so rescued, saued, and purchased for thy self. Be there no night hereafter in this place, but let a cloudles, seren, and perpetual day here raigne: and as in the seats of the blessed Spirits, the Sunne, nor *Phebe's* face is to be seen, but thou Sunne of iustice plac'd in the midst of a most bright and quiet Kingdome; spreadst round about and sendst forth a glorious light: (d) so, (I beseech thee) shine, burne, and flame forth in this little orbe of

my

my hart, O immense light, O dateles and infinit verity of my God.

(a) *Soph.* 1. (b). *Ion.* 4. (c) *Num.* 1. (d) *Apoc.* 21.

IIII. MEDITATION.

The preparatory Prayer.

Actiones nostras, &c.

The Prelvde.

T*He eyes of our Lord are more lucid then the Sunne*, (a) more bright then lightning, and yet saith he, *I wil suruey Hierusalem with lamps.* (b)

1. *Point.* Consider in IESVS his absence with how many, and what mists of obscurities, the hart of man is beset. IESVS indeed, is the true light, which illumines a like the Angelical and sublunary world. For as wel from Angelical spirits as humane

mane minds, with light diuinely ſhed, he baniſheth the darknes of ignorance, and errours; which ſhining forth anon giues euery thing it's price and eſtimation; while the good, the euil, the profitable, and hurtful, are knowne, & diſtinguiſhed as they are indeed;and laſtly thou maiſt eaſily diſcerne, whither thou art black or white, euen as the Sun ariſing giues to each thing its colours, which the darke and ſable night had confounded before.

2. *Point.* Conſider then, how powerfully IESVS, as ſoone as admitted to enter into the hart, expels & baniſheth al ſinnes from the ſecretſt nookes thereof, to wit, his moſt capital enemyes, wherewith he would not haue any thing to doe; and ſurely what ſociety can be, *between light & darkneſs?* (a)Marke this alſo, how aptly vices are expreſſed in in the formes of Serpents, owles toads, dragons, and what els, in Styx or Libia, is more vgly, foule, pernicious.

3. *Point.* Behold how the Angels are astonished, seeing those monsters of vices so detected, & chased away by IESVS: What madnes, say they, or blindnes is this of men, to suffer so importune and vicious a pest to domineer and raigne ouer them? (a) *2. Cor. 6.*

THE COLLOQVY.

LORD, how long shal the wormes of sinnes possesse and gnaw my bones, which in the accursed soyle of my hart, without seed rise vp alone of their accord? Shal these Stygian Dragons, and cruel vipers, stand alwayes before the eyes of my mind, to strike and wound my soule with

with a thousand and a thousand terrours? Shal I eternally feele that gauling prick of conscience, day & night, like furyes, to wound, to launce, and murder me outright? search very seriously, good IESV, euery corner of my hart; omit not the least path of this labyrinthian errour, where thou studiously pryest not, least perhaps some dormouse, batts, wormes, escape thine eyes. So truely is it fit thy seat should be expiated and purged from these Hellish fiends, which now for so many Ages past thou willingly wouldst haue to be dedicated and consecrated to thee.

Pater. Aue.

O beatam cordis ædem. Animose puer verre,
Te cui cælum dedit ſedē Monſtra tuo vultu terre.
Purgat ſuis manibus. Tere tuis pedibus.

IESVS SVVEEPS THE DVST OF SINNES from the hart.

THE HYMNE.

O *IESV thou art come from Heauen,*
Find'ſt lying al at, ſix, and ſeauen,
In ſeueral ſhapes, my horrid ſinnes
To ſweep away. the broome begins;
Not like the chips, when thou didſt keep
At home, and with the beſome ſweep
The duſt, and little chips, which flew
About the houſe, but now in view,
Thou ſweep'ſt, as chips cut from that tree
Which was the ſourſe of miſery,
Thoſe mōſters, loathſom duſt, where breeds
Th'old ſerpent; on this filth he feeds.
Hels Scauendger, come take thy load,
The muck, the viper, ſerpent, toad.

THE

THE INCENTIVE.

1. GOE to, you pure Inhabitants of Heauen, which ioyned prayers tire out the gracious and benigne IESVS, that he would deyne to cleanse this hart, of al its filth. For we sily dwarfs, as woulded but of slime, can neither lift vp our eyes to Heauen, nor open our lips to prayer.

2. Would any one beleeue? Oh force! Oh excesse of diuine loue! God with a secret force applyed, of holy affections, and a liuely sorrow of the mind truely penitent, as certaine besomes, conferres succours of diuine grace; where-with from the floure of the hart he sweeps out the filth of sinnes.

3. Goe on, my little IESV, and oh! expel, tread, crush vnder thy

holy feet this poyſonous virulence of ſerpẽts, which with their venome intoxicate and kil my ſoule. Deſtroy them quite, and ſo frame me a hart wholy according to thy hart.

THE PREAMBLE to the Meditation.

VVhen *Lucifer*, foyled by the inuincible forces of *Michael* (a) that great Leader of the heauenly Hoaſt, with his factious and rebellious ſquadrons, was caſt downe headlong into Hel, a new light was ſeen to ſhine in heauen, new peace to ſmile, new loues to burne, & new delights to powre forth themſelues.

Beſides, the glorious victories acheiued vpon the *Moabits*, *Iebuſæans*, and other barbarous Nations, either expulſed or els conſtreined at leaſt to pay tributes to the people of *Iſrael*, bred

bred a general peace and ioy to the whole *Paleſtine*.

But alas! the Leader of this infernal Legion, thus precipitouſly throwne downe, what a dreadful terrour brought he vnto ſea & land? For hence amid the ioyful & triumphant acclamations of the bleſſed Angels, this verſe was rung into the eares of miſerable mortals, *Woe to ſea and land, becauſe the deuil in a great rage deſcendes vnto you.* (b)

Hence truly, the open ſprings of al our euils, hence flow our teares, hence theſe ſo many ſnakes deriue their being, which occupy and ſo cruelly torture our minds. But what is this? I am deceiued. For me-thinks I ſee a huge ſhole of ſerpents, chaſed away from the lurking den of the hart. But alas! how I feare, leaſt the enemies in their flight may leaue therein ſome impreſſion or print behind them. Surely thou excellent *Dauid* didſt daily exerciſe thy ſelf, and ſweepſt thy ſpirit, as thou haſt written of thy ſelf(c) yet with al thy ſtudy and exactnes, doe what thou couldſt, thou couldſt neuer bring to paſſe, but ſome little duſt would alwayes yet remayne, or ſlimy trace be left behind, at leaſt from the trailing of thoſe ſerpents.

It is very wel: IESVS with new brooms in the Chapel of the hart ſtands ſweeping out the duſt, leaſt ought ſhould eſcape his induſtry or eyes. O admirable thing! The bleſſed Spirits, ſtand amaz'd at this, either lowlynes of mind, or officious diligence of his, and yeald him thanks for that benefit beſtowed on man. Goe to then, O thou victorious and triumphant IESVS, ſpurne, trample this Hydra, a beaſt of ſo many wicked ſerpents heads, kil him with thy flames, that hereafter he may haue no enterance or place in thy Sanctuary. And thou, moſt Bleſſed Dearling of my hart, fortify and preuent al the wayes & paſſages of the enemy, and place ſtrong Guards at the entryes and gates thereof, leaſt happily they ſteale or ruſh in any where; for they are not al of one and the ſelf-ſame kind. Some there are which like dragons with a foule & vgly flight corrupt the ayre; ſome like Aſpikes and vipers, craule on the ground, ſome ſodainly peep vp like lizards, and leap away againe; others like touds lye lurking at the very gate of the hart, vpon aduantage, yet ſlouthful the while. Theſe like bats be ſtirre themſelues by night only; they on the contrary of the race of harpyes or hauks, appeare by day, and attend their prey: So great necessity thou hast, deare soule, not to be idle at any tyme or place. Nor yet truly as soone as they are thrust out, by the powre and industry of IESVS, is al the busines quite done: For then the banished pests euen choake the aire againe with an intollerable stench, thunder & lightnings, cast forth outrageous stormes, they tumult, they rage, they mutiny, they trouble al things, and euen menace and threaten al extreamities, vnles (which they clayme as their right, and exclayme to be their due by title of victory) they may be suffred and haue leaue to returne to their ancient home, againe. But thou my sweet IESV, open the earth the while with a horrible rupture, and fold them vp with a like ruine, to that, wherein of old thou threwest to Hel the double prodigyes, those spirits, refractory and rebellions to thee

thee. And that they may neuer be ſeen or heard of more, or raiſe any new tumult, being-bound, and ſent to thoſe diſmal vaults beneath the ground, damne them to eternal darknes; that they may looſe al hope of returne againe, or raging any more. (a) *Apoc.* 12. (b) *Apoc.* 12. (c) *Pſalt.* 76.

V. MEDITATION.

The preparatory Prayer.

Actiones noſtras, &c.

FIRST POINT.

HOw fierce and cruel a warre God made in Heauen once againſt ſinne, may hence be gathered, in that he damned Sathan and his Cōplices, precipitouſly throwne downe from thoſe happy ſeates of beatitude vnto the extreame torments of euerlasting fires. How implacable a warr likewise he brought against the same very enemy on earth as easily appeares, in that he feared not to descend into the lists of this mortal life (a) that fighting foot to foot, and hand to hand, he might vtterly defeat the deuils works, to wit, sinne. Lastly, how deadly a hatred he beares in Hel to that wicked enemy, is cleere enough by this, that not enduring sinners to remaine any longer in these lists, bidding them depart, he banisheth them, into such miserable dungeons of eternal punishments.

2. *Point.* Attend besides, with what study and diligence, he commaund the monsters of vices, to pack away from our hart, like as a noble General in warr, as soone as he hath taken some Towne or fort, either by a sodaine stratagem or assault, remoues

moues the ancient Magiſtrates, and pute the ſouldiours in Garriſon from their ranck and place, nor ſuffers any one to remaine behind, that might ſtirre vp the leaſt ſparckle of any treaſon.

3. *Point* Now with what iubiley and ioyful ſignes the Angels exult and triumph in a manner, when they behold that infamous rable of portents to be thruſt forth, and chaſed from our hart! How ſtand they amazd in the meane tyme, at ſo great a multitude and deformity of enemies! But how eſpecially they admire, that infelicity or ſtupidity of ours, that we ſhould euer ſeeme to afford any place to ſuch execrable and damned Ghoſts as theſe.

(a) *Ioan.* 3.

THE COLLOQVY.

OH what dulnes of mind is this, what ſtupidity of hart, that we ſhould ſo long ſuffer theſe monſters, to reſt and abide with vs, as if they were ſome freinds and familiars of ours! Oh truly admirable goodnes of God! who hath attended and expected vs ſo long to returne to the duty and office of good men; and now at laſt moſt powerfully hath brought vs into liberty, wherefore we wil ſtedfaſtly purpoſe, and determine hereafter, to die rather, then once to afford any place in our hart to ſinnes.

Pater. Aue.

Bone IESV, fontes fluant, Illis animam mundare
In cor nostrum toti ruant A peccatis expiare
Gratiarum riuuli. Ecce gaudent Angeli.

IESVS THE LIVING FOVNTAINE IN THE HART.

THE HYMNE.

BEhold the fountaines liuing Spring:
Both here & there in Angel brings
Souls soyl'd with vgly spots within:
Oh how I now am loathing sin!
Which nought could wash but streames of blond,
That issued from Christs wounds o floud!
The sourse from whence thy torrent flowes,
Is IESVS *hart? 'tis that bestowes*
Eu'n the lasts drop, to cleanse my spots.
O scribled hart, with blurrs & blots
Of horrid crimes! wash, wash, with teares,
Thy sinnes. Thy paper written beares
Being once made white, (what doth afford,
Al ioy, content, repose) the WORD.

THE INCENTIVE.

1. IF IESVS be absent, I am arid, dry and with out iuice; so as neither I feele God, nor any thing of God. Oh cruel aridity! O fatal drought!

2. If IESVS be present, he sheads diuine dewes of graces, he opens springs of incredible sweetnes; the hart flotes only and swimes, and sincks in these torrents of celestial delights. Oh grateful dewes! O blessed springs! O ineffable delights!

3. Angelical hands lade heither those waters of life, sprinckle there-with my hart and soule, cleanse, & water them with endles springs of Paradise.

THE PREAMBLE to the Meditation.

O Holſome ſtreames of *Siloe* (a) Whereof the blind no ſooner drinke, but they preſently recouer the Light of their eyes! O powerful waters of *Iordan*, where in *Naaman* plunging himſelf, his fleſh became imediately like the fleſh of a little Child, and ſo was cleane! (b) O profoūd Spring! which ſtreaming downe in the midſt of Paradiſe, (c) thence diuides it-ſelf into foure heads, ſo many riuers, wherewith it waſheth a great part of the earth. The one called *Phiſon*, which paſſeth by the Region *Heulach*, with a moſt commodious riuer, for the vſe of mortals, waſhes and waters al the parts of the world. The other *Gehon*, paſſeth along by *Ethiopia*. The third *Tigris*, that rapid and violēt ſtreame, with ſcours the *Aſſyriās*. The fourth *Euphrates*, ſo renowned in the monuments of ſacred Writ. And oh! to

me

me ſweet waters of *Iacobs* wel! with one draught whereof the poore *Samaritan* woman (d) felt the thirſt; and head of concupiſcence ſlacked and quenched in her, which til that tyme no ſprings, nor yet whole flouds, could take away quite, or ſo much as refreſh or diminiſh neuer ſo little. Nor can I chooſe but admire thee, O prodigious ſprings, which with an endles ſtreame ſprungſt from the iaw-bone, with whoſe *Herculean* ſtrength, *Sampſon*, as armed with a triple knotted club foyled and vanquiſhed a thouſand *Philiſtins* (e) Laſtly, O thou moſt bleſſed Spring, at whoſe waters, thoſe ſo happy flames of nuptial affects, betwixt *Iſaac* and *Rebecca* (f) were anciently kinled!

But, O miraculous things! behold here from the bottome of the hart, an endles ſpring to ariſe, plenteou-

ſly

ſly watering with ſeauen channels the vniuerſal face of the earth. Behold there that maſter , pipe, more large and ample then the reſt, from whoſe head as it were eternal waters flow into the other ſix. But fix thine eyes eſpecially vpon IESVS who keeping in the center of the hart , in prodigal and profuſe vrnes or ceſterns diſtributes whole flouds of graces. Hence mayſt thou diſcerne the primary ſprings of iuſtification, to breake forth, thence more copious ſtreames of conſeruation to flow , and of the other ſide , the flux or flow of graces to ſwel againe and grow into a vaſt ſea of waters. Theſe are dealt to ſuch as firſt begin , thoſe are offred them who walke the way of perfection, others with ful channel are powred forth to ſuch as climbing the ſublime mount of vertue are got to the

the top. Casting thine eyes here also behold how in these streames of limpid, veynes, certaine little *Ethiops* (who I know not) are washed, with the ministery of Angels, and how bring cleansed, from the coale-black race of crowes they are transmitted into the candid family of doues. Come hither then you dry & thirstie soules, flock you hither: Why drinke you so long of those bloudy streames of *Egypt* ? Why carouse you so those muddy marish waters of the durty *Babylon*? Why prize you those false bewitching cups of the world, to with, that *Circean* hag? Here maist thou rather, o thou foole, drinke thy belly-ful of endlesse liuing waters; and wash if thou wilt, and rinsh thy whole mouth; with which draught thou maist put off the old man, quench, thy thirst, take courage lastly deriue thee

thee a whole streame of water *Springing to eternal life* (a) Wherefore *doe thou wash me Lord from mine iniquity*, which vow was familiar with Dauid. (h) Wash I pray and first my wil, alas! defiled with the filth of extrauagant and wandring affections ; and especially with the sordid dust of self loue. Wash my mind also, and with al wipe away al darknes of ignorance and errour from it. Wash likwise my hands, ah! (how I blush for them) so fowly dight with crimes. Wash my mouth; how I blush againe! how slow, infamous, impuden t! Wash my tongue I euen tremble to say it) so intoxicated with the poyson of scurrility and calumny. Wash my palat, alas! with sootist relishes corrupted. Wash mine eies, ouer-cast with the noxious colours of wrath and melancholy humours : myne eares , enchanted with

with the enticĩg charmes of witches, Syrens : my feet alſo ſoyled with the duſt and mire of lewd concupiſcēce: my hayr, and laſtly cogitations, for theſe alſo are in foule plight : ſo is there nothing in me that is not impure and il affected. Ah ! I dye of thirſt, and deſire of thy loue ! Oh quench and extinguish the thirſt, the heat of my dying hart ! O eternal loue ! inexhauſtible Spring ! But your, thrice happy Cittizens of heauen, o glorious Angels, who as certaine riuers flow from this fountaine of al good, receiue and ſhut vp firſt with ful minds the whole ſpring it-ſelf, them in the open lakes of your harts, plunge this my dry and thirſty hart, drowne it in the ocean of loue. So I coniure your by that very loue, which is the immenſe ſpring and fountaine it-ſelf, from whence you haue taken both your nature and ſpirit, of whoſe draught you ſtil liue, and ſhal liue, as long as Eternity laſts: very happy and bleſſed. (a) *Iohn.* 9. (b) 4. *Reg.* 5. (c) *Gen.* 2. (d) *Ioan.* 4. (e) *Iudic.* 15. (f) *Gen.* 24. (g) *Ioan.* 4. (h) *Pſal.* 50.

VI. MEDITATION.

The preparatory Prayer.

Actiones noſtras, &c.

FIRST POINT.

COnſider ſinne to be a true leproſy: for as this infects and fouly ſpots the body; ſo that vitiates and corruptes euery part of the hart and ſoule; and though the act be paſt, yet leaues a foule and vgly blot behind it.

2. *Point.* Conſider further, this moſt vgly & foule blot is not waſh-

ed

ed away, but with the bloud of the only immaculate Lamb: which neither the ſacrifices or ceremonies of the old Law, nor faſts, nor other auſterities of this kind can wipe away without the ſprinckling of this bloud: *For without bloud, remiſſion is not had.* (a)

3. *Point.* Conſider laſtly, that as heretofore the poſts and threſhal of the houſe being ſmeared with the bloud of the Lamb, with held the ſword now drawn and ready to ſtrike, of the ſmiting Angel, from killing them in the houſe by a death ſo ſtudiouſly prepared (b) ſo with this bloud, al helliſh power is expelled, and reſtrained, that thoſe wicked foes of our ſaluatiō may not touch the very entrance of our hart, or dare ſo much as looke vpon it: Laſtly as the Preiſtly robes, yea the Sanctuary it-ſelf was ſanctified and hol-

hollowed by the bloud of the Lamb (c) ſo beleeue from the bloud of Chriſt al ſanctimony (d) deriues into our minds. (a) *Heb* 9. (b) *Exod.* 12. (c) *Exod.* 29. (d) *Heb.* 9.

THE COLLOQVY.

L*Ord wash me againe, from mine iniquities, and cleanſe me from my ſinne.* (a) Waſh the mind, and let al the clouds of ignorance vaniſh quite. Wash the wil, and purge il appetits conceiu'd from the falſe nuages of tranſitory things: wash the memory, and wipe away ſelf-loue growing, from an ouer-weening of my ſelf, and my own doeings.

Cleanſe my feet, hands, eyes, and tongue, nor let any thing remaine in me, that is foule and polluted, or wich may any wayes offend thy Maieſty, neuer ſo little.

[a) *Pſal.* 50. Pater. Aue.

Eia IESV tibi notum
Cor ſi lubet, luſtra totum
Pia tuo ſanguine.

An non cernis! toto patet
Ara cordis, nil te latet:
Foue tuo lumine.

7

IESVS PVRGETH THE HART WITH expiatory bloud.

THE HYMNE.

O Hart lie open freely take,
These sprinckled drops, enough to slake
The flames of lust and quench the fire,
Of hel it-self, O Hart desire
Thy Lord, now is he entred in,
To put to flight the deuil sinn,
The world the flesh: Behold h'is gone,
Thy contrite hart. plow'd, harrowd, sown,
May, watered with his heauenly dew,
Spring forth, and fructify anew:
To which annex some pearlik drops,
That thou with ioy maist reap thy crops.
Raine followes wind: sigh, teares begin,
And drown as with a deluge sinne,

THE

THE INCENTIVE.

1. ALthough the hart be vnworthy and wholy vncapable of ſcore of celeſtial graces, yet IESVS howſoeuer, of his ſoueraign goodnes, powrs thereon and ſprinckles it at leaſt with ſome little drops thereof, to inſtil thereby into the ſoule the firſt loues of heauen, and to excite a thirſt thereof.

2. Behold in IESVS abſence, how dry, dul vntoward, poore, miſerable the hart languiſheth and pines away; how the Angels likewiſe ſcanding round about, and ful of horrour, are amazed the while, & with reuerence are praying to IESVS to be moued at ſo great a miſery of the humane hart.

3. Goe to then, water, water, O moſt ſweet IEVSV, this vnhappy

hart: ſprinckle it at leaſt with ſome little drop of the ful fountaines of thy ſweetnes. It is now enough, ſweete IESVS; for loe the hart came preſently to it-ſelf againe, as ſoone as it felt but one little drop of thy diuine loue to be ſprīckled on it.

THE PREAMBLE to the Meditation.

M*Oyſes*, it is to no purpoſe to take the aſperſour in hart (a) and with a purple thread to tye the yſop ſo about it; with which dipt in the bloud of the victime; thou buſily purgeth the Altar, the volume of the Law, the whole people, attentiuely liſtning to the ſtatutes and precepts of God: this ſhed & ſprinckled bloud, wil not expiate ſinnes, nor to the Tabernacle or Leuits afford any ſanctity a whit nor wipe a-

way

way the ſpots of leproſy, nor cancel the ſtigma or ſeared print of ſinne; vnleſſe with al thou reguardſt this fountaine, this bloud, which alone can waſh away the monſtruous ſordidues and which ſhed on the tree of the Croſſe yeald life to ſoule imparts a candour and beauty to them, and that like to the ſunne, which in the ful of the Moone, powres forth his light vpon her orbe and to ſick mortals makes her more amiable. Nor truly for ought els that water and bloud ſo flowed from the ſide of dying IESVS; then to ennoble ſoules, being cleanſed with that purple to waſh their robes, to make them fit and apt, that crowned with victorious laurels they may eternally triumph, with the immaculate Lamb.

Take therefore O IESVS, loue of my ſoule, from this infinit bath of thine ſome few little drops, at leaſt, and ſprinckle thy Sanctuary therewith, I ſay, the ample field of my hart; whoſe ſhure poſſeſſiō, thou haſt taken to thy ſelf long ſince. But you, O ſmitting Angels, goe farre away hence, the houſe is marked already, the ſignes of Tau is printed on the doores: be-gone I ſay; for where this marke is ſeen, it is a crime to enter in. Oh would to God, my IESVS dearely beloued, with *Dauids* feruour, I could pray and obtaine this fauour at thy hands.

Lord blot out my iniquities, wash me yet more from my wickednes, purge me of my ſinne. Thou shalt, ſprinckle me with yſop, and I shal be cleane, thou shalt wash me, and I shal be whiter then the ſnow. Turne away thy face from my ſinnes; and blot out al my iniquities. Create in me, O God, a cleane hart, and renew a right ſpirit in my bowels. (b)

Let

Let there be no corner , I beſeech thee , which thou purgeſt not no portion of my ſoule , which thou bleſſeſt not with the fruit of thy pretious bloud. The ſwallow with her owne bloud reſtores ſight to her bling yong ones. The bloud of a Goat expels al manner of poyſon. Againe, the bloud of doues, let forth beneath the wings , quickens the dulled ſpecies of the eyes: nor is it fit my God, nor iuſt that from thy precious bloud, my hart ſhould not feel likewiſe the ſame effects. The bloud of victimes ſhed from the ſacrificed Holocauſts , bred no corruption, nor ſtench, nor flyes, that ſordid creature , but rather euen deſtroyed thoſe importune and irkſome things. The Sacrifice at *Bethel* (c) offered vp by *Iacob*, they ſay, was ſo purely and holily performed that not a fly diſquieted the Patriarch:

buſy in this rites. I wil not, Lord I wil not haue my hart a *Bethanues*, or Temple of *Bel* (d) a peſtered with flyes, and ruining al with filthy & corrupt goare: where *Belſebub* (e) giues forth his Oracles, and exhibits himſelf, awful and terrible to men, in deſpaire of their ſaluation. How I hate theſe direful and dreadful Sacrifices, theſe rites! Thy bloud, O ſweet IESV, is alwayes red with purple, and white with lylies intermixed. (f) For theſe two colours thou affect'ſt, the purple red, & ſnowy vhite; wouldſt thy Cliens, and deuotes addicted to them, and to be known by them. This bloud of thine, to thirſty ſoules quenches their heat, to hot and toyled ſpirits ſends a humid breath; to broken and diſmaid harts, giues fortitude and courage.

(a) *Exod*, 24. *Heb.* 9. (b) *Pſal*. 50.

50, (c) *Gen.* 35. (d) *Ose.* 10. (e) 4. *Reg.* 1. (f) *Cant.* 5.

VII. MEDITATION.

The preparatory Prayer.

Actiones nostras, &c.

THE PRELVDE.

IN the midst of the Temple, was placed a huge brazen vessel, whēce many channels yssued forth, apt to communicate their waters, for the vse of Preists and Leuits, wherewith they washed themselues when they went to sacrifice. (a)

Weigh the munificence of God, who thought it not enough, for declaration of his famous and good wil towards vs, to water the hart of man with his owne bloud, vnles he left vs also a fountaine famous for ſeauen channels, from whence the guifts of graces might plentifully & prodigally flow into our minds, to wit ſeauen Sacraments inſtituted to this end, to waſh vs, to expiate our ſinnes, and to wipe al ſteynes from the hart.

2. *Point.* Conſider the grace, which flowes from the fountaines of the Sacraments, to be a golden water, which turnes al it touches into gold; and that ſo powrefully and diuinely, as there is not the leaſt action of our life (ſo it be ſprinckled with the liquour of diuine grace) which we ought not to make more reckoning of, then of al the treaſures and riches of the world; as meritorious and worthy of eternal happines.

3. *Point* Conſider now, how al graces, & merits depend of the only Sonne of God, and thence are deriued by certaine pipes or aqueducts

as

as from the rock or head of theſe liuing waters: Wherefore we are moſt ſtudiouſly to receiue and keep this liquour of grace; leaſt any whit thereof ſhould breake from the bancks of our hart; nor is any occaſion of heaping merits to be omitted, which we greedily reach or catch not at. (a) *Exod.* 3.

THE COLLOQVY TO the wounds of our Sauiour.

MY ſoule, O God, hath thirſted after thee; (a) vnles thou repleniſh it with heauẽly waters, who ſhal recreate or refreſh it? My ſoule is blacker then a coale; (b) who ſhal waſh it whiter then ſnow, (c) vnles thou powreſt forth thy grace into it, which clearer then any chryſtal, fals from the ſtreames of thy ſide, hands, and feet? Oh ſacred ſprings of *Syloe* (d) infuſing light to the blind! Oh Springs of *Elim*, which refreſhed the heat of the people of *Iſrael* (e) dying nigh with thirſt, amid thoſe parched ſands of that vaſt deſert! Oh rock (f) ſmit cruelly with the tongue and hand of the Sinagogue! a rock, I ſay, not exhaling flames of fire, but powring out aboundant ſtreames and flouds of benedictions; which with a continued courſe, accompanyed the pilgrime people into *Paleſtine*. Oh you holſome *Iourdan* waters of *Naaman* (g) flow with a copious channel into my hart, that no locks or ſluce at any tyme may hinder your courſe. But your, O you heauenly Miniſters of God and mans ſaluation diue and plunge in this fountaine placed in the midſt of the houſe of God, thoſe *Ethiops* our minds, I ſay, ſo vgly and deformed

med with the wretched colour of vices; that by your meanes, being rised and cleansed once they may issue forth like doues. Amen.

Pater. Aue.

(a) *Psal.* 62. (b) *Thren.* 4. (c) *Psal.* 50. (d) *Ioan* 9. (e) *Exod.* 15. (f) *Exod.* 17. (g) 4. *Reg.* 5.

Quis hic vultum non serenet?
IESVS ecce sceptra tenet
Cordis in palatio.

IESV tantum ora pandas
Manda quod vis, da quod mandas
Adsumus obsequio.

8

IESVS RVLES AND REIGNES IN THE louing & deuout hart.

The Hymne.

O Mightie Soueraigne, if you please,
To deigne a looke & view our seas;
Where harts like ships with wind & tide
Are sayling; some at anker ride,
Some with waues and boystrous windes
Tost to & fro; 'mongst them you find
My floating hart, with euery blast
Of greife or of affliction past,
As 'twere immersed with in the maine.
But yet, Greate Monarch, if you deigne
To be my Neptune, or to guide
The sterne of my poore hart, beside
The surges flying ore my decks,
Reigne in my hart, let Hel play reks.

THE INCENTIVE.

1. VVhen IESVS ſits in the hart, as in a Throne & there commands, the hart is a Paradiſe, our cogitations, affects, deſires, are euen as Angels, Cherubins, yea Seraphins, ſo here doe al things burne with diuine loue.

2. God raignes nor rules not? Sinne therefore ſwayes and beares the rule, moſt tyrant-like; and ſtrikes and wounds the miſerable hart, already ſtretched on the cruel rack and torture, with terrours, ſcruples, horrid ſpectres, beſtial appetits: no hart, but euen a Hel.

3. Little King, great God, tame my rebellious hart, ſubdue it to thy heaſts, and eternally commaund it: Surely I wil doe what I can to dedicate and conſecrate it to thee: doe thou defend the place, wherein thou likeſt wel to be ſhut vp.

THE

THE PREAMBLE to the Meditation.

THe pacifical *Salomon* in those dayes of old had built him a Throne of iuory [a) six degrees or steps in height, on both sides whereof watched a Lyon, very exquisitly wrought, the truest symbol of regal Maiesty; and likewise for the people beneath in the midst of the Temple he erected a very eminent and stately Chapel. And so to thee Immortal God; the heauen is a Throne the earth a foot-stoole. For thou sit'st (as sacred scriptures (b) tel) vpon the wings of Cherubins, whence thou giuest Oracles, prescribest lawes to the world; and euen with the only looke, maiesty, and state, becomst most terrible to the haughtiest mīds. Hence thou exactst iust punishments from

from the damned : hence thou inebriatst the blessed Citizens of Heauen , with the nectaral honey of thy goodnes: lastly hence thou carrousest cups mingled with the gal of iustice, and honey of pure goodnes , to the earth , suspended betweene heauen and hel. Besides in the triumphant Church the celestial spirits , whom we cal Thrones , are thy royal seat; and in the militant , the sacred Altar is thy lodging chamber, where thou sweetly takest thy rest.

But nothing is thine owne so much or due vnto thee, with a better title, then the hart of man, which with a low abasement of thy self, and a singular obedience to thy father, thou hast lawfully recouered and bought with the price of immense labour and paynes ; yea redeemed with thy bloud, & a shameful death on the Crosse. Here , o pacifical

Salo-

Salomon, thou rulest, here thou commaunds with a beck, in this soyle or seat, as in thine owne dominion, thou swayst in that manner, as there is none so bold or of so impudent a face, that dares, vnbidden, step in a foot, or, not touched with the point of thy golden scepter, (c) looke in a-doores. Here thou hearest the humble suits, and petitions of thy subiets, here thou stiflest lewd desires, putst a bridle on the rebellious senses, tamest the insolence of carnal concupiscence, sweetnest the acerbity of labours. And, (O most happy kind of gouernment!) thou alone sufficiently fillest the whole hart, attended with a most happy trayne of heauenly Citizens which thy retinew or Court can neuer depart from thy side, or vanish from thine eyes; so strongly tyest then the minds, harts, and loues of al vnto thee

thee. Moreouer in the basis or foundation of this royal edifice, stands faith, more cleere then any Chrystal; in which glasse of Eternity, mans hart sees and beholds the past and future things. The whole frame susteines it-self, on that, thy surest and most constant truth; wherewith thou proppest and holds it vp. For if faith leane not vpon thee, it cannot hold the name or dignity, of faith. Now the steps by which they ascend into this Throne of the hart, are those which the Kingly Prophet insinuats, where he sayth: *They shal passe from vertue to vertue.* (d] Humilitie lyes in the lowest place, obedience followers, anon pietie ariseth then patience shewes it-self; resignation attends and perseuerance tops and crownes them al. The foũdation faith consists of Iaspar, each stair shines with his special gemmes.

The

The first, is black with ieat, the second, greene with the emarald, being the colour of hope, the third glissens with the purest chrystal, the fourth is hard with the adamant, which no contrary violence or force can master; the fift euen sprinckles fire with the chrisolite, but the Carbuncle, the sixt, flashes forth both fire and flames at once: yet thou midst al, my sweetest IESV, o prodigy! not only sits secure, but euen deliciatst thy self.

There are besides, two litle columnes or pillastres of this Throne; loue appeares on the right hand, and feare of thy iustice is to be seen on the left: yet sitst thou so venerable with diuine Maiesty, in this humane seat of the hart; as the face of thine enemies, cannot behold the dignity of thy countenance, or endure thy aspect. There thou giueſt precepts, and art preſently obeyed; commaundſt, and thy heaſts performed in a moment. The Angels themſelues, euen the Cherubins and Seraphins, tremble to approach any neerer; as who know wel enough, this litle region to be properly thine, ſo only made for thee, and ſo due to thee by right of purchaſe, as whatſoeuer is leſſe then thee, or ſhorter then eternity cannot pleaſe or ſatiate the hart; grown proud of ſuch a Lord. For it is hungry and thirſty, nor liues contented with any owner, vnles thou fix the ſeat of thy kingdome in its precincts. If thou beeſt preſent with it deſires no more; if abſent, come in al created things at once, & wooe it neuer ſo much, there wil yet be place enough for more. If thou getſt from thence, al felicity departs with thee: if thou abideſt, al beatitude

comes

comes ſodainly thither. Raigne therefore, and eternally raigne in my hart, O loue of my hart. Quiet the motions of perturbations, nor euer ſuffer the vnhappy hart; to thruſt the King out of his ſeat; then which cannot happen a greater diſaſtre to it. Nor ſuffer I ſay, o darling and delight of my hart, that one hart ſhould be shared into many parts. For thou ſuffereſt no riual. Oh ſuffer it not euer to be enticed with the allurements of worldly pleaſure, which gate being once ſet open, I ſee how eaſily the enemy wil rush in. Be thou to it a brazen, yea, a wal of fire, which may ſo roundly girt the Tower, as that no paſſage may be found vnto it. But that only the Holy Ghoſt may come downe from Heauen, whereto the hart lyes open and enter therein, with a ful gale and occupy the whole hart; that

that ſo I may truly profeſſe and glory, *My beloued to mee and I to him.* (e)

(a) 3. Reg. 10. (b) *Pſal.* 17. (c) *Eſter,* 5. (d) *Pſal.* 83. (e) *Cant.* 2.

VIII. MEDITATION.

The preparatory Prayer.

Actiones noſtras, &c.

The Prelude.

MY *Kingdome, is not of this World,* (a) for my Kingdome is thy hart, o ſoule deuout to God.

1. *Point.* Conſider how God ſeemes to make but litle reckoning of the rule, and gouernment of heauen & earth, in regard of the dominion and care he hath of mans hart; wherein, as in a breife epitome or abridgement, he ſumms and collects togea-

togeather the whole perfection of the Vniuerse.

2. *Point.* Consider againe, how sweet the yoke of Christ is; compared with the most cruel and direful tyranny of the deuil. For into what horrible vices and abhominations, doth not this wicked Tyrant and cruel butcher of soules, drawe men who are subiect to him? How farre this Lord differs from the genius of the world. For if this Impostour promise mountaynes of gold to his clients and followers, after a long & irksome bondage, after a tedious yoke, and loads of intollerable iniuries, which it layes vpon them, it really performes nothing but smoak of words & empty shadowes. Lastly, how diuerse this Masters benity is from the hard & cruel apprentiship of the flesh, which for a singular reward of most abiect seruices, re-

payes

paies nothing but a thousand sordities, and miseries, as wel of the soule as body.

3. *Point.* But on the contrary, where IESVS rules in the hart, the appetits, which were before vnbridled, comply with the law of reason, and the soule-it-self, reduced as it were into the forme and order of a watch, being in tune and wel disposed, poyseth al her thoughts, words, and works, with iust weight and measure.

THE COLLOQVY.

SHal be with the most sweet IESVS, earnestly beseeching him he would take ful possession of the hart, commaund therein, as in his Kingdome, and exercise an ample power vpon al the faculties of the soule: that he would aduance

uance, pul downe, enrich, impouerish; lastly fraue it to each beck and signe of the most holy and diuine wil.

Pater. Aue.

Sunt auscultent qui Platoni,
Aut facundo Ciceroni,
Aut Mundi stultitiæ.
Tu ne verba vitæ sperne
Audi Patris æternæ
Dicta Sapientiæ.

IESVS TEACHETH the deuout hart.

THE HYMNE.

O IESV speake, thy seruant heares,
But thou must find me pliant eares,
For of it-self my hart and wil
Is seeking drops that doe distil
From a limbeck that's rais'd on high
With streines of wit, which soon are dry.
Oh let me heare what thou dost speake
(Peace) in my hart! Ah, if it leake,
As doth a vessel pierced through,
It naught auails to heare. For how
Can I retaine that in my breast,
Except some heat of grace digest?
Oh with thy lessons that impart!
With thee Ile soone get al by hart.

THE INCENTIVE.

1. BEhold here my litle Doctour teaching from the pulpit of the hart. O speaches al of milk! O nectar! How affectiously the speaches? With what a grace he teacheth! How ioyfully the hart leaps, while it takes the words of eternal life.

2. Like Maister like Scholer; especially if he take delight to hang on the lips of God, instructing as a Maister; and with prompt and ready eares and mind but drinck his inspirations. Here truly he playes not the mans, but teacheth the Angels part, yea is indeed a very Angel.

3. Diuine Doctour, teach me to doe thy most holy wil, euery where and in al things; for I require no more. I shal sure be wise enough, when thou alone shalt tast and relish with me.

THE

THE PREAMBLE to the Meditation.

THe tyme wil come, o delight of my ſoule, O Spouſe of bloud, (a) when mount Caluery ſhal be thine Accademy, thy diuine humanity, thy booke; for woden Chair, the hard Croſſe, where this volumne ſhal be laid vpon, for points, ſtripes, Laſhes for commaes, for Auditary of ſo diuine a Maiſter, the wicked Iewes. Al men ſhal read in that book, and if they mark, vnderſtand, how potent thou art, who canſt ſo aptly linck togeather, things by nature ſo farre diſtant from each other; life with death, folly with wiſdome, pouerty with riches, ſtrength, with weakenes, gal with hony, high with low. Here the diſciples of the Croſſe ſhal learn;

with what pretty ſlight of thy wiſdome, the moſt tender worme [b] of thy humanity hanging on the line and hooke of the Croſſe hath drawne out of the bowels of mens harts, that horrid and cruel fiſh *Leuiathan* (c) and cruſhed his head: with how vnvſual an inſtrument, the engine of thy humility, thou ouer-threweſt that mad Tower of *Babel*, brakeſt with thy meekenes the adamantin hart of the Iewes, how with thy admirable ſweetnes and affability, like that worme (which ſeemed a prodigy to Ionas) (d) thou didſt ſo ſmit the root of that flowriſhing iuy, as ſuddenly al the leaues withered, that is the ceremonyes of the ancient Sacrifices were aboliſhed, Altars demoliſhed, the preiſtly and regal power of the Iewes, the ſplendour of that flouriſhing nation, in times paſt, withe-

red

red like a tree ſtrooken and blaſted from heauen. Laſtly in this open and vnfolded book, al poſterity ſhal acknowledge what were thoſe ancient mercies, of thine, (e) hidden hitherto in the immenſe treaſures of thy bowels, and euen the Gentiles themſelues whom the diuine goodnes might ſeeme to haue caſt off for ſo many Ages paſt, ſhal now behold the moſt abſtruſe ſecrets of the higheſt things, hidden heretofore. But now, [moſt louing Doctour) doe I ſee another. Schoole ſet open to thee, the ſpacious Galery of man's hart, a noble Lyceum, wherein thou Lord and Maiſter teacheſt the ſoule, thy diſciple within and inſtructeſt her with the precepts of thy moſt holy wil. Speake therefore, I beſeech thee Lord, the eares of my hart are open, ſpeake O loue of my hart, for thy words *are ſweeter then the hony , and the hony-comb* : (f) *milk and holy vnder thy tongue , the hony-comb distilleth from thy lips*. (g) Oh fiery words of loue ! Strong , efficacious , endles , thundring words, which impetuously throw al things to the ground , ruine Ceders , fetch vp mountaines by the root , reare the lowly hil lying in the plaines strengthen collapsed minds , dash and crush the proud : Lastly ; words of a most indulgent Parent, teaching his dearest child al manner of holsome precepts. Lend thine eares then my hart; God is he that speaks. Heare my Child (for so IESVS aduyses from the pulpit of the hart) doe thou giue thy self to me : Let me be thy possession, thy nurse , thy food , for nothing can satiate thyne appetite without me. My Child, throw away those leekes and garlik of *Egypt* , turne thy face from the stin-

ſtincking waters of pleaſure , and put thy mouth rather to my ſide, the wine-cellar of graces, whence at eaſe thou maiſt draw and deriue to thy ſelf moſt soueraigne and incomparable ioyes : For ſake thy ſelf and thou shalt find me ; leaue the vayne contentments , of the ſenſes, and thou shalt purchaſe to thy ſelf thē ſolid & ſincere delights of Heauē. Learne of me,child, not to build thee worlds,or frame new Heauens, nor to worke wounders , (h] but learne that *I am meek & humble of hart.* (i)Be alwayes mindful of benefits beſtowed vpon thee; for nothing ſo exhauſts the riuers of diuine grace, as the blaſting vice, of an vngrateful mind. Be preſent to thy ſelf follow thine owne affairs , ſquare al thy actions to the exact rule of reaſon, and perſwade thy ſelf this , and haue it alwayes in thine eyes , that thine;

and the felicity of al rests in me the only soueraigne good. (a) *Exod.* 4. (b) 1. *Reg.* 23. (c) *Iob.* 40. (d) *Ion.* 4. [e) *Psal.* 88. [f) *Psal.* 18. (g) *Cant.* 4. (h) *Aug. serm.* 10. *de serm. Dom.* [i) *Mat.* 11.

IX. MEDITATION.

The preparatory Prayer.

Actiones nostras, &c.

THE PRELVDE.

THey *shal be al docible of God.* (a)

1. *Point.* Consider how Almighty God, from the first creation of things, hath proposed al his perfections to be openly read in the book of creatures. (b] For by the ample spaces of Heauens, he hath manifested his immensnes; by the diuersity of celestial influences, the variety of his guifts and graces; by the splendour of the sunne & moone, his

his beauty; by the admirable viciſci-tude of the ſeaſons of the yeare, his prouidēce; by the immoueable firmnes & ſtability of the earthly globe, his conſtancy and immutability, by the plenty of his benefits wherewith he hath moſt copiouſly endowed vs, his goodnes; Laſtly in the huge vaſtnes and depth of the ſeas, he hath left the inexhauſtible abyſſe of his eſſence expreſſed as it were in a painĉted cloth.

2. *Point.* Conſider beſides by what meanes the ſame God heretofore hath explicated his myſteries to vs, with diuers Oracles of Prophets, & with the manifold ſhadowes and figures of the old law. (c) So the greene buſh [d) vntouched in the flames, ſignified the virginity and fecundity of the Virgin-Mother. The brazen Serpent (e) with whoſe aſpect, erected in the wildernes, were

cured the wounded, ſlung with ſerpents, expreſſed the Croſſe, & death of the ſonne of God, to be the holſome remedy of miſerable mortals. The mariage ſolemnized betweene *Salomon* & the Egyptian, womã (f) & repreſented the hypoſtatical vnion of the eternal Word with the humane nature.

3. *Point.* But while theſe things ſeemed but ſmal to the great immenſity of his loue, he himſelf being made man, came downe vnto vs; and taking poſſeſſion of the hart; and aſſuming to him the office of a Teatcher, inſtructs it, and deliuers the art, not of working miracles, nor of building new worlds, but imbuing it with new precepts and altogeather vnheard of hitherto. *Learne* ſaith he *of me, becauſe I am meek, and humble of hart.* (g)

4. *Point.* I wil endeauour to giue

my

my mind very frequently and seriousl̄y to learne this lesson by hart, wherein consists the summe of al Christian perfection, and I wil examine my self how diligētly hitherto I haue behaued my self therein, and what method I wil afterwards keep to be exact.

(a) *Ioan.* 6. (b) *Sap.* 13. *Rom.* 1. (c) 1. *Cor.* 10. *Heb.* 11. [d] *Exod.* 3. [e] *Num.* 21. (f) 2. *Reg.* 11. (g) *Mat.* 11.

THE COLLOQVY.

SHal be directed to the Holy Ghost, most earnestly crauing him to afford me light to comprehend the diuine mysteries; a hart docile & apt to receiue such lights and motions; strength of memory, least the species of things once receiued may easily vanish away; and force sufficient wherewith to execute what I shal thinke fit to be done.

Pater. Aue.

Sume IESV penicilla,
Cordq; totum conscripilla
Pijs imaginibus.

Sic nec Venus prophanabit,
Nec Voluptas inquinabit
Vanis phantasmatibus.

10

IESVS PAINTS THE IMAGES OF THE LAST things in the table of the hart.

The Hymne.

O Rare Apelles; *loe the fraine,*
My hart; but first prepare the same,
Which is al slubbered'ore with sinne,
Wipe al away, and then begin
To draw the shapes of vertue here
And make the foure last things appeare;
That no Chimeraes of the brayne,
Or Phantasies I may retayne.
Besides vouchsafe to draw some Saint,
Begin, sweet I E S V, *figure paint,*
Whom I may imitate, and loue,
As did Narcissus. *From aboue*
Descend Apelles, *thou diuine,*
Come euery day and draw some line.

THE INCENTIVE.

1. NOthing is more miſerable then the hart when it giues licence to wandring imaginations, and liberty to ſelf loue. My God! what images! what phantaſies! what enormityes! what folies are depainted there!

2. But after that IESVS, the diuine Painter, hath entred into the ſhop of the hart, & taken the hart it-ſelf as a table to draw and paint therein, thou maiſt ſtreight diſcouer the image of God and Trinity reformed; the effigies of IESVS, and MARY drawne, the whole celeſtial Court repreſented, and the face of the gallantſt vertues expreſſed; whether with greater luſtre of colours, or feeling of piety, or delectation of the mind I can not ſay.

3. O

3. O moſt louing IESV, imbue my hart with the colours of Heauen, paint not ſhadowes, but genuine and natiue images, ſnowy innocence, greenes of hope, the pureſt gold of charity; that ſo the cloſet of my hart may come to be a certaine Cabinet or Reliquary of al perfections.

THE PREAMBLE
to the Meditation.

MY hart (my IESVS) is an emptie table, ſince thou haſt wipped away thence the images and fading ſhadowes of worldly things, and throwne downe the idols which I my ſelf had wickedly erected in thy Sanctuary; take then, I pray, thy pẽcils in thy hands, and dip them in the liuelyeſt colours thou haſt; that no ſeries or tract of

yeares,

yeares , nor inclemency of the ayre, nor dust raised from the earth ; may blemish or deface what thy al-working hand from the most absolute idæas of the eternal wisdome, hath diuinely painted. For thou , o great Artisan , hast set downe in writing with thy hand , those noble soules, *Abraham*, *Isaac*, *Iacob*, and the rest of the family of the predestinate. Thou truly , art that admirable Authour , who didst put the last hand to the azure orbes of Heauen, appliedst the purest gold to the Starres; the greenes of the emerald, to the herbs , the snowy candour to the lillyes, the crimson to the rose, the purple to the violet , pale with yellow mixed. Thou sprinckleſt cristal on the adamant , the etherean brightnes, on the saphir, the Vulcan flame; on the carbuncle : Lastly, thou hast endowed al things, as wel sen-

ſenſible as inſenſible, with ſuch variety of colours, and ſweet delectation as the eye cannot be ſatisfied with beholding them. (a)

And in this huge vaſtnes of the world, my God, thou haſt ſhewne thy omnipotence, which the eye of the mind may wel admire, though not conceiue or comprehend but in the diuerſity of created things, which a ſtrange knot, concording diſcord, and diſcording concord moſt ſtreihtly tyes together: thou haſt impreſſed the liuely image of thy infinit wiſdome in the order of this vniuerſal Al; but there is not among al thy creatures any one, no not the leaſt of them, wherein conſpicuous draughts of thy goodnes, ſhine not euery-where. Since therefore my hart is a void table, already fit to be wrought, draw I beſeech thee diuine Painter, and here deli-

neat

neate only these foure images, which deuouring tyme with no age may cancel or were out. And first frame in this table, that last grimme, and dreadful line or period of my life, and let these here be the draughts of this sad image: Let me lye as dying, with eyes sunke into my head, with pale and deadly face, leaden lips, let death stand by threatning with a terrible iauelin in hand, here the deuil menacing with weapons of temptation, there the Guardian Angel breaking his thrusts, in my defence. Aboue be the Iudge seen attending the passage & issue of the soule, let the children houle at the doleful bed; the seruants, each prouiding for himself: adde, if thou list, the coffin lying not farre off, wherein the senselles corps is to be laid, vntil that day, whē the last trumpet's sound shal sumon the buried to arise.

Oh

Oh holſome and profitable Picture! whoſe only aſpect wil ſhew me that is, my nothing, to my ſelf; and laying the ſwelling winds, wil hold me in my earth, that I grow, not proud yea wil giue me a generous and ſtout hart, that triumphantly I may trample on the trash and trumpery of the world, and creeping on the ground with frequent ſighes preocupying death, before my death mount vp to heauen.

Now pious IESV, I pray draw, and finish alſo the other part of the table, of the other ſide, with due lineaments. Be that maieſty ſet forth, wherewith as Iudge thou shalt appeare one day, and be ſeen of al to handle and diſcuſſe the cauſes of the liuing and dead: let me here behold thee ſitting in the clouds, with the mouth armed, with a two edged ſword, and with an eternal ſeperation

peration ſeuering the sheep from goats. On which image as often as I shal caſt mine eyes, I may feele the bit and feare of thy dreadful iuſtice caſt vpon me, whenſoeuer I shal lash out like a fury, into the precipices of vnbridled appetites.

Goe on heauenly Artificer, now muſt thou, paint a Hel, that lake ſo dreadful for its ſulphur and flames, where the vnhappy ſoules cheyned together, with howling and diſpa-ring cryes fil al things, and with that tragedy publish their wretched-nes, and miſerable condition. So exhibit the whole, as I may ſeeme to behold the vncleane ſpirits, touch the darknes ſelf as with the finger, feele the gnashing of teeth, heare the horrible blaſphemies, their cries, their pathes, their flegme which in vaine they caſt forth againſt God, their bans and curſings, wherewith they

they cruelly teare one another, that being astonished with the sight of this picture, I may eternally sing thy mercies, (b) which hath held me vnworthy a thousand and a thousand times, from this lamentable abysse of infinit euils.

Lastly, my good Painter, looke where the rest of the ample space of my hart, seemes void, I say not expresse, but shadow, I pray, the image at least of eternal glory and beatitude. Exhibit howsoeuer which a rude draught that house & royal seat, where thou layst open the most diuine treasure which thou hast reserued for thy children, with the title of inheritance. Here let that great and blessed City of celestial *Hierusalem*, built al of gold (c) and precious stones, euen dazle the eyes; there let the Citizens of heauen be ſeen clothed with the ſunne that graue Senate of Patriarchs and Apoſtles, with heads crowned with golden diadems, beſides thoſe valiant Heroes, who with the price of their bloud and life, haue purchaſed themſelues immortal laurels. Figure alſo that mount, purer then chriſtal, wherein the candid mother of the lamb, and the reſt of the virginal flock deliciat with the Lamb himſelf, amid the chaſt delights and Quires. (d)

Now then that theſe foure pictures may the better be conſerued, let them not be encloſed I pray in Moſaical work with certain litle ſtones linked and cimented togeather, leaſt perhaps diſagreeing with themſelues they fly a ſunder, but let one be ſet in ebony, another in cypres wood, the other be garniſhed round with plates of ſiluer, al enameled and ſet with

with topase stones ; and finally the last be deckt with the richest gemmes. Take off thy hand now if thou please, the worke is fully finished. Yet one thing more remaines, my diuine Painter, of no smal reguard, forsooth, that to thine exquisit work thou adde a curten, least vnluckily the dust, or moister ayre, or more vntoward mind, may euer taint or least obscure so elegant and terse a picture. (a) *Eccl.* 1. (b) *Psal.* 88. [c) *Apoc.* 21. (d) *Apoc.* 14.

X. MEDITATION.

The preparatory Prayer.

Actiones nostras, &c.

THE PRELVDE.

I Would to God they would be wise, & prouide for the last things. (a)

1. *Point.* Consider IESVS to be an excellent Painter, who with the only pencil of the mouth, to wit, the draught of one litle word of *fiat*, painted the whole world with so great and artificious a variety of colours; and how in each creature he hath expressed very excellent lineaments of his power, wisdome, and goodnes.

2. *Point.* Thinke what force hath the liuely image and representation of death, perticular iudgement, and Hel, to restraine the lawles liberty of our life and too excessiue mirth; and how much the remembrance of the heauenly glory preuayles to stirre vp the mind in the course of vertue, and to take away the difficulties they vse to meet with, who walk that way.

3. *Point.* Thinke this also with thy self, how the pictures and the images of the foresaid things expressed, at

no tyme, ſhould be wiped away from the table of the hart, this being the ſourſe of al our teares and errours, to be ſo careles and backvvard to conceiue and premeditate before hand, vvhat is to be exhibited in the laſt act and period of our life.

(a) *Deut.* 32.

THE COLLOQVY.

SHal be made to God, beſeeching him not to ſuffer, that either the delights and honours of the vvorld, or proſperity & aduerſity may euer raçe out of our minds thoſe pictures, vvhoſe affect is ſo neceſſary for vs to our Saluation.

Pater. Aue.

Bone IESV conde crucem
Virgam lanceamq; trucem
Conde in imo corculo

Nulla præualebit lues,
Amuleta quando strues
Hoc myrrhæ fasciculo

IESVS BRINGS IN THE CROSSE INTO the hart, and easily imprints it in the louer.

THE HYMNE.

HAst thou no Harbinger to bring
Thy furniture, so great a King,
But must thy self in person come
To order al, and hang this roome?
My hart alas! it hardly brooks,
To be transfixt with tenter hooks;
For nayles and hammer, now I see,
And ladder, al prepar'd for me.
Ah! without sheets I see thy bed;
Thy Crosse, no bolster for thy head
Except it be a crowne of thorne,
Thy canopy is Heauen forlorne.
Al things lament thy paynes to see,
IESV come in, I'l mourne with thee.

THE INCENTIVE.

1. GOe in louely Crosse enter launce, spunge, nayles, scourge, bloudy, thornes, get you in to the Closet of the hart. Welcome stil, but on this condition that IESVS bring you in himself; for mirrh with IESVS, is admirable, and meere sweetnes.

2. Thou saist thou louest IESVS; then needes must thou his Crosse: for if otherwise thou boast to loue IESVS, thou deceiuest thy self and others.

3. Most sweet child; what haue you and I to doe with this lumber here? scarce art thou come into the world, but thou art oppressed with the weight of punishments. Oh plant thy seat in my Hart! and then shal I chalenge Hel it-self: for if

IESVS

IESVS and I hold togeather, what *Hercules* can ſtand againſt vs both?

THE PREAMBLE to the Meditation.

MOſt worthy Painter, I pray, take the table in hand againe, for before thou, makeſt an end of thy worke in the eſcuchion of my hart, thou muſt needs paint thine armes, with ſome motto or other that by the deuiſe thou mayſt be known to be the Maſter of the houſe.

The Palaces of Kings, and their houſes, as wel in the Countrey as Citty; euery-where are wont to giue forth their titles, armes, and names of their Anceſtours, to wit, the monuments of their royal ſtock and ancient nobility. As for thine armes and tropheues of thy name good IESV; I take them to be thy Croſſe;

nailes, laũce, crown' of thornes scourges; that Pillar whereto thou wert boũd; & those very cords, wherewith thou wast tyed. I (sayd he) haue, been trained vp in labours frõ my youth.

Goe to then, for my sake, among those foure images of the last things, which thou hast fully finished in al points, let these instruments, as Tropheye of thy Passion, be likewise pourtraited. The Crosse would be of Cedar, that is painted in his proper colour; the speare sprinckled with bloud, the nayles dipt in the same dye, the pillar marked with drops and streakes of bloud; lastly, the cords and scourges with bloud also, but so as waiht away with teares here and there they make certain distinctions between. At sight of these armes, if they offer to encroch or approach neerer to the hart be the enemies dispersed; and fly as wax before the face of the fire. But ho! my Lord, print I pray that Crosse more deep into my hart; if it be churlish & resist, vse violēce with it & soften it if need be; if with too much softnes it proue il and diffuse it-self, constraine the parts, to consist and hold together; but be sure that euery colour thou here workest with be wel mixed with thy bloud, for this colour pleaseth best, as being the simbol of loue. Be this Crosse to me sweet IESVS, as a buckler, to rebate and blunt the weapons of the enemyes: be it a wal, or trench to girt me in; armes for me to assaile my enemyes with al, may it stirre in me alwayes, first a fresh and liuely memory of thy passion, then a burning desire of suffring with alacrity for thee al hard and cruel things; no otherwise indeed then of those thornes were roses the black-berries; the whitest-lillyes: let this wood, cast into my-mind , turne the bitternes of the waters, into sweetnes (b) change gaul into hony, alloes to sugar , Let the Crosse be the mast of the sayling ship , wherein transported I may happily land at the hauen of saluation ; my bed ; where couching as the Phenix in her nest, and consumed with the flame of loue, and turned to ashes I may dye *Iacobs* ladder (c) to mount to Heauen by; the Pilgrims staff to passe the Iourdan (d) the sheep-hooke,to keep in the straying senses in their dutyes; Pharus whereto I may direct my course in the tempestuous Sea of the world, amid the thickest fogs or fowlest weather. May the launce and scourges strike a terrour to the proud and rebellious spirits , that menace a far-off , and reuewing the assault by fits try to inuade thy Sanctuary. Pitch Lord , and plant this

this Croſſe of thine in the turret of the hart;be it there a ſtandard,which being aymed at , as the Captayns ſigne and ſigne of warre, may al the faculties of my mind anon, be ſummoned with alarmes , and pel-mel directly rush vpon the enemy.Being armed with this Croſſe as with the keeneſt ſword , I may cut off the wretched head of the cruel *Holofernes* (e) and riſe vp againſt my Aduerſaries , like that Angel , who in a night alone foyled & vanquished at once, a huge army of the proud (f) *Senacherib.* Wherefore auant you hellish troops , packe hence away, & fly vnto thoſe darkeſome vaults. There is none of you that dares abide before the Tower of the hart, where the armes of the Supreame Numen are now ſet vp : in ſight whereof the Angelical ſquadrons ſtand in battle array; where not only horrour and dread but imminent & most present ruine waits vpon you. For death himself at the sight only of the Crosse, turnes his back; sinne also takes his flight a long with him, and both togeather with their common Captain Sathan the deuil, in great dispaire tumble headlong in the lowest Hel. (a) *Psal.* 87. (b] *Exod.* 5. (c) *Gen.* 28. (d) *Gen.* 32. (e) *Iudith.* 13. (f) 4. *Reg.* 19.

XI. MEDITATION.

The preparatory Prayer.

Actiones nostras, &c.

The Prelude.

P*Vt me as a signe vpon thy hart.* (a) Be thou as wax, for euery forme; I vvil be the seale, and imprint the armes of my passion in thee.

1. *Point.* In the cōquered & vāquished Tower of the hart the victorious Iesus, placeth the trophies & triumphs of

of his paſſion, forſooth, as Lord and Maſter of the place, leaſt any one hereafter may chance to chalenge it to himſelf, or ſeek to inuade it.

2. *Point.* There can be no ſuch force or power of tẽptations, which vvith the liuely apprehẽſion of theſe armes may not vtterly be defeated; no aduerſity ſo great, which may not cheerfully be borne; no ſuch alluremẽts of worldly pleaſures; which with a generous loathing may not be reiected.

3. *Point* How happy the ſoule which is nayled with Chriſt vpõ the Croſſe! how rich, while vnder that wood are found to be the riches of Heauen & earth! how defenſible & ſecure againſt al the power of Hel, being the impregnable Tovver of Chriſtians, whereon a thouſand targets hang (b) the whole armary of the ſtrõg, either to endure the shock of the enemyes or to aſſaile them. (a) *Cant.* 8. (b) *Cant.* 4.

THE

THE COLLOQVY.

SHal be made by turnīg the ſpeach, by way of Apoſtrophe, to al the ſymbols of Chriſts Paſſion, as nailes, lance, vvhips, and alſo vnto Chriſt himſelf, crauing moſt earneſtly of him, as wel to conſerue in our minds the memory of thoſe things which he hath ſuffred for our ſakes, as to admit vs into the ſociety, and communion of his moſt bitter chalice; that we may alſo merit one day to enioy our part of glory & eternal felicity.

Pater. Aue.

Euge puer, rosis pinge,
Latus hoc, et illud cinge,
Totum cinge corculum,

Sparge fœtus verni roris.
Sparge totā meßem Chloris
Sternis tibi lectulum.

13

THE HART CONSECRATED TO THE loue of IESVS is a flourishing garden.

THE HYMNE.

IESVS, *thy power and gratious wil*
Is alwayes drawing good from il,
And life from death, and ioy from grones,
And Abrahams *childrẽ makst of stones.*
Behold a quick-set is my hart,
With thornes and bryars on euery parte;
One drop of bloud alone thou shedst
Wil make a rose, wheres'er thou treadst:
Oh may my hart sweet odours breath
Of vertue! Ah! thy thorny wreath
That pearc'd into thy brayne made red
And purple roses on thy head.
Then for my sinnes, that I may mourne,
With roses grant a pricking thorne.

THE INCENTIVE.

1. IF IESVS, be in thy hart, thou needst not feare, the vnlucky accidents of man's life, for he of very thornes makes sweetest roses.

2. The most sweet odour of the white & ruddy rose, which IESVS is, recreates and refreshes men and Angels, kils the rauenous fowles. Hence when the hart with IESVS is beset and closed, in with roses, sinne and the deuil get them far enough; for they cannot abide the smel of them.

3. Wilt thou be a soft couch, wherein litle IESVS may like to repose and rest in? let the Hart be crown'd with the roses of vertues with the snowy flower, of innocence, with the purple of patience, and breath the frangrancy of true deuotion.

Here

Here IESVS feedes (a) here he ſleepes. (a) *Cant.* 1.

THE PREAMBLE to the Meditation.

O*Vr litle bed is flourishing* (a) *our garden* likewiſe is al beſet with flowers. Here the ſweet ſmelling balme exhales an odoriferous breath here amid the ſnowes of lillyes, the roſes grow al purple; here Cinamon with ſafron, caſſia mixed with mirrh, haue a fragrant odour with them; there is nothing here that breathes not admirable ſweetenes to the ſmelling. Come therefore, O loue of my hart, my beloued, that feedſt among the [b) lillyes, who delightſt in flowers, come into the ſweet delicious bed, or rather, if thou wilt walke the ſpacious allyes of the orchard and in the walkes. Oh

Oh my Sun, dart thofe fruitful rayes of thine eyes, and with thy fweeteft breath more gentle then *Zephirus*. infpire an odoriferous foule into the flowers, wherewith my hart being hedg'd in, like garden-plot; euen fmiles vpon thee. Here the humble violet, fairer for her lownes, euen wooes thee with her foothing flatteryes, the higher fending her odours as fhe ftoopes the lower; a noble fymbol of a lowly mind; which vertue; as a firft begotten daughter thou haft kiffed from the cradle and tenderly embraced, Here the lilly rifing fomewhat higher, from the ground, amidft, the whiteft leaues, in forme of a filuer cup, fhewes forth her golden threads of fafron in her open bofome; a noble Hierogrifike of a fnowy mind, a candid purity, and a cleane hart, which now long fince haue been thy loues : for hence that ſtrange obſequiouſnes of thine in thoſe thy yonger dayes , ſeeking and complying ſo with thy Virgin-Mother.

Here now beſides the pourpourrizing roſe , the flower of Martyrs dyed with the ſanguine tincture of their bloud , repreſents that incredible loue which put thee (o loue piouſly cruel !) and nayled thee on the Croſſe; ſo as it is leſſe to be wondered, it ſhould dare ſo afterwards to caſt the martyrs into flaming furnaces, into cauldrōs of melted lead, into burning fires , with liuing coales; load them with Croſſes gibbets, puniſhments , and take away thoſe actiue ſoules , which yet theſe generous and noble Champions , very willingly lay'd downe of their owne accord. Here alſo that bitter mirrh, but bitter now no more , whoſe chiefe force conſiſts , in preſeruing bodies bodyes from corruption; distils those first (c) teares of hers more bitter then the later ones that follow after; but so much sweeter, as more powerful: This shewes and represents those teares, sighes, pressures, labours, which thy dearlings, Confessours, Mōks, Anchorites, haue taken voluntarily vpon thē, while in the doubtful course of this life the pious Pilgrims hyed them to the heauenly countrey.

But, O most sweet IESVS to rauish thee aboue the rest with admiration, and his loue, the heliotropion of my hart, that flower, the genuine image of the Sun conuerts it-self to thee; whom therefore so assiduously it followes, for hauing so from nature such, a hidden force and sympathy with that eye of the world, the parent of al light. In this flower doe nestle harts enflamed with thy loue, whose

voyce

voyce is euen the very ſame, with that of thy *Spouſe; My beloued to me, and I to him.* (d) Deliciate thy ſelf then, IESV the delight of my hart, amidſt theſe amenityes of flowers, and from thoſe fragrant & odoriferous garden beds, let the bleſſed Spirits thy companions weaue them coronets, & delightful garlands, more pleaſing, I dare ſay, to thy diuine Maieſty, then thoſe of old, ſo offred vp in Lachary (e] wherewith the head was deckt of the ſonne of *Ioſedech*, the high-Prieſt. Yea wil I be a little bolder with thee; doe thou thy ſelf, my I E S V, from thy Garden gather & pluck thee flowers, make thee poſyes, wreath thee chaplets, and doe your Angels only help the while. My litle I E S V S firſt ſhal chooſe the gathered flowers himſelf, then ſhal you bind them vp with a golden thread, & laſtly he with theſe flowers

theſe

these wreaths, these chaplets shal compasse in the hart about, that with this preseruatiue and odour of these flowers, he may banish from the mind al contagion that may vitiat or infect.

Goe to then goe on you blessed Spirits, but I pray giue him the rarest flowers into his hand, euen the pride and honour of the eternal spring; which neither heat of sunne may fade, nor tempest or showers deface nor obscure the lustre, beauty or dignity, which the diuine graces prodigally haue powred vpon them.

(a) *Cant.* 1. (b) *Cant.* 2. [c) *Cant.* 1. (d) *Cant.* 2. (e) *Zach.* 6.

XII. MEDITATION.

The preparatory Prayer.

Actiones nostras, &c.

THE PRELVDE.

OVr *bed flourisheth*, ſaith the Spouſe. (a)

1. *Point.* Conſider IESVS to be truly a *Nazarean*, that is flowry or flouriſhing; for the loues to be conuerſant with the ſweet odours, and flowers of vertues. Wherefore I wil ponder, how grateful it is to him to repoſe and reſt himſelf among the lillyes of purity and chaſtity; the roſes of martyrdome and mortification, the violets of humility and prayer; the Sunne-affecting marigolds, that is, the noble ſoules, and pliant to euery beck, of the diuine vvil;

wil; and other garden plots, of the rest of vertues, with whose loues, he is so taken, as that euery-where, at al occasions, he sents their odours and hunts after them.

2. *Point*. These flowers should neuer fade, with any weather, not with the parching heate of the sunne, I say should not wither with the heat of carnal temptations, nor hang the head with the southerly wind of austere sadnes; nor pinched vvith the cold and frozen blustering of the north, that is, not nipt or blasted with the euil breath of dulnes in spiritual things: but should rather be continually watered with the dew of celestial graces, and from the substance of the hart, deuo'yd of al corruption, draw and deriue their iuice & bloud, where by they might prosper and flourish euermore.

3. *Point*. I vvil seeme to behold

the litle IESVS, ſporting in this litle flovvry garden of the hart, picking here and there, and plucking with his hand, now thoſe flowers; the Angels remayning aſtonished at ſo great familiarity, and adoring the vvhile. But for me I wil reſolue vvith my ſelf, to keep eſpecially the liily of chaſtity inuiolable, vvithout the leaſt ſtaine or blemish of its candour.

(a) *Cant.* 1.

THE COLLOQVY.

TO the moſt Bleſſed Virgin, Mother and Diſciple of al chaſtity, of vvhom I vvil craue the meanes firſt to keep chaſtity, and then earneſtly beg her help and patronage, to vanquish eaſily al the temptations of the fleſh.

Aue maris ſtella.

Cor exulta, quid moraris
Gaude plaude inuitaris
Pijs IESV cantibus

Sonat chelys Angelorum
Sonant tubæ Beatorum
Mixtis IESV vocibus

13

IESVS SINGS IN THE QVIRE OF THE hart, to the Angels playing on musical instruments.

THE HYMNE.

IF thou within my hart wouldst dwel;
O IESV, then what Philomel,
Could warble with so sugred throte,
To make me listen to her note?
The Syrens of the world to me;
Would seeme to make no harmony.
When they a long, a large resound
Of pleasures, thou dost them confound,
Chanting a long, a large to me,
With ecchoing voyce, Eternity!
A briefe of pleasure, with like strayne
Thou soundst a long of endlesse payne,
The Diapason, ioyes for me,
To liue in blisse eternally.

THE INCENTIVE.

1. VVhat doe me heare my hart, what doe we ſeeme to heare. How ſweet are theſe rapts? how ſweetly this celeſtial harmony enchants the ſoule, and rauiſheth it quite beſides himſelf. Oh happy houer! O happy lot! when I E S V S and the Angels ſing in parts, to the melody of the Heauens.

2. When the hart ſweetly reſpires, it ſighes for and after, IESVS, and chants forth his praiſes with a gladſome ſpirit. O muſike. O incredible conſort! I heare me-thinks the Quires of celeſtial ſymphony to ſound; and ſee my ſelf in the midſt of celeſtial ioyes.

3. *Let thy voyce ſound in mine eares* (a) my Beloued. For to ſpeake in a ward, moſt humbly proſtrate at

thy feete, I here, proteſt;that neither I doe nor wil euer loue any other then the ſweeteſt dolours and paſſions of IESVS. Away with theſe flatteryes of ſelf : Away with theſe bewitching Proſtitute of carnal pleaſures , Syrens auaunt with your alluring charmes of my affections, Let IESVS only ſound in mine eares. *For his voyce is ſweet and graceous his face.* (b)

THE PREAMBLE to the Meditation.

O Sweet harmony! O diuine confort! Or are we mocked the white ? I heare me-thinke a lute, the harpe playes, the flutes and cornets wind, a whole Quire is kept in the hart; and if I be not deceiued it is a ſong of three parts ; they ſeeme to play according to the number of the

the muſitians that play. For the Angels here of th'one ſide, though they vſe diuers inſtruments; yet ſounding but one thing ſeeme to play but one part; then IESVS the skilſul and moſt exquiſit Muſitian tunes his voyce, and beares his part; laſtly the hart hath his. For amidſt theſe numbers it ſings and dances al at once. How quaintly and aptly the ſtrings, wind inſtruments, and voyce al agree: With how admirable a pleaſure the numbers quauer and iump with al. But then how noble a Hymne is ſung the while how curious & elegant IESVS ſtands in the midſt, not only a ſinger, but as a Rectour of the Quire alſo with a magiſtrat rod in hand now lifted vp, and then let fal; keeping the time, and ordering the key and ayr of the whole ſong. If you aske me the ſubiect of the dicty the Royal Pſalmiſt [a) had designed and penned it long a goe, when he sayd : *I wil chant the mercies of the Lord for euer.* For to this purpose IESVS the prime Christ, records his ancient loues to the humane hart, & now mixing with admirable skil flats with sharps, sharps with flats, the tenour with the base, & running diuersly diuisions he touches with a sweet remēbrance now vvith a moderate, novv remisse, now slow, and novv vvith a quick voyce, the innumerable number of his benefits vvhere-vvith heretofore he hath vvooed the hart : Wherefore recording things in this manner, novv he stirres vp pious desires, vvhich he had often enkindled before, novv vvith a grauer tone, he exaggerats the horrid feares of sinnes, and hel, vvhich he not rarely had inculcated heretofore, and novv againe vvith a sharper streyne of the voyce, cal he to to mind the liuely and ſudden impreſsions of compunction for ſinnes, the agitations and excitations, of the mind, determining a change of life, nevv vndertakings of great things, heroical entrepriſes, and a thouſand other of the ſort; vvith vvhich diuine loue is vvont to play and dully in the harts of louers. Meane vvhile the Angels tune their inſtruments and ſtrings to this argument, and while themſelues for aſtoniſhment cannot open the mouth or expreſſe a word; they betake them to their inſtruments, and apply al the induſtry and art they haue to play vpon them, and with a ſacred ſilence, tacitly admire the diuine mercy towards men and euen with the geſture of this dumb admiration moſt vehemently ſtirre vp and incite themſelues to magnify and extol the praiſes of God to the Heauẽs: whoſe manner is and cheife delight, to rescue mortals from the iawes of hel, to put the burning coles of diuine loue the cold, tepid, and slouth ful minds, and with water as it were to extinguish the flames of libidinous lust. Lastly with one glance or cast of the eye, as with a thunderbolt to ruine and depresse the proud and haughty and for the humble and modest, with the only beck of his wil to raise them sudenly. But what doth the hart while, in whose musike roame is al this harmony made? Now it dilates it-self, now contracts, now it riseth, now fals, it feares, it hapes, it loues, it hates, it composeth and wholy frames itself and al it's appetites to the rules, numbers, and sweet modulation of musike.

Then truly it obserues and clearly discernes the difference between the celestial

celeſtial, that true, ſtable, melodious muſike, and the falſe voyces, the harſh, the trembling, the broken, & vngrateful tunes of the world. For tel me I pray, what is that bewitching, or, as you cal, delicious muſique of the world, but confuſions of *Babel*, mad baulings, ſtrãge clamours, vnquoth noyſes? One ſings the perilous tops of dignities, the ſmokes of honours, the vncertaine degrees of Magiſtrates, the vayne breath of popular glory: another with a ſordid mouth ſounds for the obſeene and foule delectations of the fleſh, beſtial delights, wine, feaſts, and banckets: another ſings outrage in's angers: another with a fayned voyce diſſembles, choler and rancour, harbouring within. Some like rather to flatter, as *Syrens*, ſome with ſinging to plot and couer guile and deceit. Thus are al the ſongs of the world but

but a hydeous and tumultuous noise, no harmony; inarticulate and hoarse murmurs, no musike; or if a harmony it be, it dulles truly as wel the hearers as singers; and euen kils with the very absurdnes thereof, since peace indeed cannot rest with the wicked (b) nor any quietnes be among tumults, nor tranquility, nor calmes, amidst the black, & hydeous stormes and tempests of malice. Whereas on the contrary, heauenly musike delights the hart, wipes away troubles and tediousnes, composeth the euil motions of the sick mind, repels the force of the enemies lastly puts Sathan to flight, as heretofore was signifyed in *Dauid*; who restored *Saul* to his wits againe being taken and vexed by an euil spirit, with the only playing on a harp. [c)

Now therefore my hart (for now remaynes thy part) sing a ioyful and trium-

triumphant ſong. Io, liue IESVS Victorious, liue he foreuer: liue IESVS the triumphers, the terrour of hel, & father of life. Liue IESVS the Spouſe of Virgins, the Doctour of Prophets, the fortitude of Martyrs. Liue IESVS Prince of Heauen and earth, IESVS triumph, the only poſſeſſour of my hart. Let IESVS, I ſay, liue; raigne, and triumph eternaly.

(a) *Pſal.* 88. (b) *Iſa.* 48. (c) 1. *Reg.* 16.

XIII. MEDITATION.

The preparatory Prayer.

Actiones noſtras, &c.

First Point.

I Wil conſider a triple muſike, wherof the firſt is heard in Heauen, the ſecond in earth, the third in the hart of man, deuout to God. The first truely, the Angels, frame of three parts, the Cherubins, Seraphins, Thrones, sing the treble, who with a most high and shril contention of the voyce, chant the diuinest things, the eternity of God, his immensity, power, and the rest of the diuine attributes. The Vertues, Dominations, Principates, in a certain midle tenour are occupied in proclayming the mysteries of grace, the Incarnation, of the Sonne of God, his virginal Natiuity, Passiõ, Death, Resurrection, Ascention. Lastly the Principates, Archãgels, Angels, with a graue and lower tone, sing the creation and conseruation of the world, and the rest of this kind.

4. *Point.* Attend now to the other musike, made on earth, proclayming the diuine praeyses, which is the order, symetry, and apt agreement of al

al the parts of the world, with and among themſelues; in which Quire, the foure elements with an harmonious diſcord play their parts admirably together. The Heauens likwiſe make vp the conſort, while they declare the glory of God to the whole world, *for neither are the Words or ſpeaches, whoſe voyces, may not be hard.* (a)

3. *Point.* The third ſymphony is held in the Temple of mans hart, and then is that melody made, when al the faculties of the ſoule, contayne themſelues vvithin their parts and functions; vvhen reaſon playes the treble, the inferiour appetite beares the baſe, when our wil agrees with the diuine and ſupreame wil: and ſuch is the ſweetnes of this harmony, as fils he mind with immenſe pleaſure. And no maruel, while IESVS himſelf moderats

derats al this musike with his most certaine and temperate rules and measure.

(a) *Psal.* 18.

THE COLLOQVY.

TO the blessed Spirits, whom I wil inuite, first, to sing prayses to the Diuinity: then wil I also stirre vp my self to accommodate my voyce with theirs: wherefore with al the endeauour of my mind, wil I sing with them this diuine verse, *Lord thy wil be done as in Heauen, so in earth.*

Pater. Aue.

Pulsa chordas, sonet chelys,
Dum nos recreas de cœlis
IESV cordis gaudium:

Dulce melos intonabunt
Nuum nobis excitabunt
Angeli tripudium.

14

IESVS THE SONNE OF DAVID, PLAYES ON the harp in the hart, vvhile the Angels sing.

THE HYMNE.

VVhen IESVS *doth my hart inspire,*
As Orpheus*, with his tuned lire,*
The trees with power attractiue drew,
My hart deep rooted (where it grew
In baren soyle without content)
So powerfully he drawes, that rent
From thence, it followes him, takes root,
And so self-loue, which had set foot
Is banished farre, who charm'd before
My hart deluded. Euermore
IESV *be al in al, my part,*
My God, musitian to my hart,
And harmony, which solace brings
Ah touch my hart, & tune it's strings.

THE INCENTIVE.

1. IF IESVS touch alone and mooue affects, which are the ſtrings of our hart, good God! how ſweet, how diuine a muſike he makes therein. But if ſelf-loue once play the Harper, and medle with the quil, and touch the ſprings but neuer ſo litle, ah me! it is a helliſh horrour, and no muſike.

2. When IESVS with a ſoft modulation ſteals into my hart there is ſtreight ſuch a ſweetnes in the marrow and bovvels, as al things ſatisfy and pleaſe alike; life, death, proſperity, aduerſity: You vvould verily ſay my miſeries were charmed by IESVS and his Angels.

3. Touch but the harp, litle *Dauid*, giue it a lick vvith the quil, tvvang that only, I ſay, tvvang the

domeſtido nestical harp but neuer so lightly, whereon thy Gransier *Dauid* playd so long a goe, and it is enough. It was it dispersed the horrid clouds of sadnes and melancholy, & draue away the wicked Genius. O God, when I heare this *Dauid* both father and sonne of the Royal Psalmist, playing on his harp, how my hart iumps the while, yea how ready it is to leap out of it-self.

THE PREAMBLE to the Meditation.

THe heauenly *Dauid* in the midst of the Hale of the hart, with nimble fingers, tickles the harp, to the musical numbers. Come hither Angels, then come you deare soules to IESVS, come you al: Cleare vp your voyces, and tune them to the pulse, and harmony of this harp.

This

This ſound, beleeue me, wil baniſh Sathan, and throughly purge away melancholy, that grateful ſeat of the wicked Genius.

But why the harp (moſt ſweet IESVS) rather then another? Yet ſhould I thinke thou takeſt it not by chaunce: Vnles perhaps it be that the forme and ſound of this Inſtrument. Ah! thou wouldſt preſent that figure which in mount Caluary thou actedſt ſo long a goe; playing the Chorus of that ſad Tragedy, in the publike Theater of Heauen & earth, in view of al? Ah, now I remember how thine armes and feet were then ſtretched forth on the tentours, as in the harp the ſtrings are wont. How ſtiff were then the nerues and ſinewes of the whole body: But here loue playes the harper, and yealds ſo forth a ſound moſt like the harp, reaching farr and wide, as

farre

farre I ſay, as the higheſt, midle, & nether orb extend heauen, earth, & hel. Sathan felt thee harper, and maugre al his power was conſtreyned to compreſſe his foaming anger, and bridle his implicable fury. Death lurking at the gates of hel, felt the fatal point of his dart (being no leſſe then ſinne) to be ſudenly rebated. But with vs now at the ſound of his harp, the rocks being riu'd & ſplit, began to fly aſunder, harts harder then adamants to ſoften, wicked men touched with the prick of conſcience to confeſſe their crimes, to knock their breaſt, the proper ſeat of the penitent mind, and to giue forth theſe words, moſt ful of compunction, *Truly the Sonne of God was here.* (a)

Yea the ſound went vp to Heauen alſo; and ſudenly ſtayed ſo the hand of the diuine *Nemeſis*, menacing eternal

eternal ruine and calamity to men, and now ready ſtretched ſorth to make a ful reuenge of al, as that by and by the ſame being voluntarily vnarmed, and now as the caſe were altered quite hath giuen place to mercy, which hitherto had layne hid.

But why doe I cal theſe things to memory? who knowes my hony IESVS, whether, with this harp thou playeſt not ſome-what els? What? I know not Vnles perhaps with this ſweet harmony of ſtrings thou wouldſt ſignify the ſweeteſt and ſinccreſt pleaſures, wherewith thou woeſt and courtſt the harts of pious men. For who are able to ex-preſſe with what deliciouſnes of thy pleaſing tunes thou recreatſt now and then, and erecteſt minds afflicted with the irkſomnes and tediouſnes of a wretched and miſerable life?

And

And for that we ſeely men, are altogether vnable, goe on, o you Angelical ſpirits , and here ſing againe a new mottet of thankſgiuing in our behalfe.

But you get you hence and farr enough , you gloſing dangers foule *Sirens* : Get you hence vncleane wicked and deceiptful world : I hate your rimes , your idle ſonnets ; for your , muſike lines are nets , your notes, ſnares, your voyce the foulers whiſtle. I curſe and deteſt theſe cunnings tricks. Your bals and reuels are the Theaters of impudent & infamous ſcenes; I execrat and deteſt theſe Masks and mummeryes.

Therefore , o my hart , liſten I pray , and when thou heareſt the voice of thy God, anon being ſtruck as it were and ſmil , giue a ſound with al , and attemper and ply thy voyce to his , make his wil and mine

to

to iump and ſympathize together: take heed thou yealdſt not a ruſtike muſike; and a harſh vngrateful tone; ſing to the numbers right, and dance with al whether aduerſity maane thee , or proſperity play with thee. But eſpecially lend thine empty eares to the moſt ſweet ditty of the diuine Harper : who ſweetly allures thee a farre of, and neerer hand puls thee vvith the ſound of his harp. *Come*, for ſo he ſings, *come my freind come and thou shalt be crowned with the head of Amana, with the top of Sanir and Hermon; from the lions dens, from the hils of Libbards.* (b] Take here the crowne of flowers, which thou haſt wouen for thy ſelf, fetched from the higheſt and ſteepeſt mountaines tops not with out much labour and ſweat receiue the reward of the trauels and combats, which thou haſt fought: the prize of the victory vvhich vvith taming and binding the lyons and beares, those vnruly beasts of thy passions thou hast most gloriously purchased. This harmony of IESVS singing to the hart, my soule, vvil procure there light, and gentle sleeps and imbue the vvhole breast vvith the nectar of diuine consolations, that thou maist not feele the acerbity of molestations, vvhich are necessary to be drunke by mortals. Strike out therefore thy harp most strongly, my beloued, there shal no murmure at al obstreperate and dul thine eares; the closet of my hart is vvholy vacant, that naught might hinder the svveetnes of this harmony. And you againe good Angels, tune your voyces to the sound of this harp, and I the vvhile from my immost bovvels vvil sing these verse of the Psalmes. *I wil blesse the Lord at al times, his praise be alwayes in my mouth.*

(c)

(c) For he hath taken compassion on me of his great mercy, he hath blotted out my iniquities. (d) He hath deliuered my soule from death (e) He hath crowned me in mercy and good workes, He hath replenished my soule in good things. (f)

(a) *Mat.* 27 *Cant.* 4. (c) *Psal* 33. (d) *Psal.* 50. (e) *Psal.* 55. (f) *Psal.* 102.

XIIII. MEDITATION.

The preparatory Prayer.

Actiones nostras quesumus, &c.

FIRST POINCT.

CONsider how easy and expedit is the contemplation of spiritual things, when IESVS borne of the true stock of *Dauid*, playes the harper, in the hart, and with the soũd of his diuine instrument driues away the wicked ſpirit; euen as heretofore his great Grandſier Dauid, reſtrayned the intemperance of *Saul*. Attend beſides how ſeriouſly the Angels accommodate their voyce to the ſound of the harp; that euen looke what they ſee IESVS to doe for our good, they endeauour to doe alſo, ſtudying to accommodate themſelues to our occaſions.

I. *Point.* Conſider IESVS hanging and nayled on the Croſſe ſeemed to haue caryed the figure of a harp with him, which being playd on, gaue forth as it were ſeauen ſounds, very ful of hidden myſteries and the firſt ſtroke truly of his myſtical harpe was: *Father forgiue them, for they know not what they doe.* (a) When he held vp and ſtaid the making of the world from falling, being then on the point to demoliſh quite, and with it's ruine ready to ſwal-

ſwallow the impious Parricides of God. But, o moſt vnlucky ſtroke? in the laſt ſtreyne a ſtring broke and ſnapt aſunder, and the ſoule & body of the moſt bleſſed IESVS being diſſolued, the whole harmony of *Dauids* harp was vtterly marr'd, which yet a litle after the parts being reſumed and handſomely vnited together, ſo newly rayſed againe ſung forth a triumphal ſong.

3. *Point.* Conſider when IESVS is preſent what great feſtiuityes are made, what diuine rayes doe ſhine, what plenty of graces are powred forth, and what true and ſolid pleaſures abound: but in the contrary IESVS being abſent what hydeous darknes ouer-caſts the minds, whole ſquadrons of calamities, troubles, deſperations, feares, mourning, tediouſnes ſlouth, moleſtations, and what not? come ruſhing in by troops.

(a) *Luc.* [illegible]

THE COLLOQVY.

SHal be directed to the Blessed Virgin, of whom, with the greatest endeauour of an earnest and submisse mind that may be, I wil craue leaue that what she led before, I may sing after her: *My soule doth magnify the Lord*, (a) especially since the benefits I receiued from her sonne are likwise infinit; & I wil further inuite not onely the Angelical spirits to sing; but al created things whatsoeuer, with that Psalme of Dauid: *Praise the Lord al you nations.*

(a) *Luc.* 1. (b] *Psal.* 116.

Pater. Aue.

Frustra Boreas minatur Dum in corde lectum strauit
Frustra fulmen debacchatur Atque sponsus dormitauit
Frustra spumant cœrula Tuta ridet sponsula

15

IESVS RESTS IN the louers hart.

The Hymne.

BEhold my hart doth Christ enclose,
While he doth sleep I doe repose:
As I in him, he rests in me.
If he awake, I needs must be
The cause, that made the noise within;
For nought disquiets him but sin.
But I with crosses, soon am vext:
With iniuries and cares perplext,
And I, who should my wil resigne,
Am soone disturb'd greiue, fret, repine:
Til IESVS *doth his grace impart,*
Who giues repose vnto my hart;
O happy hart, with such a guest,
Which here hath what he giues thee, rest.

THE INCENTIVE.

1. SO long as the hart in God, and God reſts in the hart (which is wrought with a holy conſent of wils) let the Heauens thunders and lighten, the earth quake, and moue out of its ſeat, the elements tumult, the winds of temptations rage and make a hurly-burly; yet the hart ſhal be quiet and laugh at al.

2. When thou haſt receiued IESVS, taking the venerable Sacrament of the Euchariſt, take heed thou awake him not delicioully ſleeping there, either with the hydeous noiſe of outrageous choler or with the obſtreperous clamour of the other paſſiõs, or by any other way of breaking ſilence, ſo much as with the huſh only.

3. But doe thou ſleep, my litle IESVS, and (as thou liſts thy ſelf) take thy reſt, in Gods name: We make thee a couch ready in the hart, we intend to loue none but thee we, wil neuer breake our faith with thee; though the winds bluſter and ſeas rore neuer ſo much.

THE PREAMBLE
to the Meditation.

I Sleep and my hart wakes: (a) It is the voyce of the moſt louing IESVS. Whiſt therefore you Heauens, earth hold your peace. IESVS ſleeping in the bed of the hart, ſweetly reſts. You buſtle in vaine, o reſtleſſe winds. The hart where IESVS takes his reſt is ſafe enough the ſhip is now in the Hauen, which the Maſter-hand of ſo diuine a Pilot guides. Ceaſe Aquilo,

Ah thou cold, gelid, cruel ſtranger of the North; bridle thy moſt ominous blaſts, for thou exhauſts and dryeſt vp the riuers of celeſtial graces freeſeſt the harts of men, with a ſlouthful yce, and nigh killeſt them with cold; thou ſtrippeſt the trees of fruit and leaues, makeſt the earth euen horrid with hoary froſts and winter downes, daſheſt the talleſt ſhips and the beſt man'd, and ſinkeſt them in a fatal gulf.

Ceaſe thou Southern enemy, Stormy Auſter, froward, hot rhewmatike (and which is worſe) thou inceutiue and fire-brand of luſts, bridle thy fatal breath wherewith thou burneſt al things, ſtirreſt humours, extinguiſheſt the fires of diuine loue; ſprinckleſt the nerues and ſynnews, diſhartneſt minds, and makes them languiſh.

And doe thou ceaſe likewiſe, ſwee-

ſweeping faune or ſcourer of the eaſterne coaſts, thou fatal African not only familiar with tempeſt, but ful of a peſtilent and blaſting breath thou ruſtleſt here in vaine, thou ſhalt neuer shake this hart, wherein IESVS takes his reſt.

But thou the fauner of the Eaſtern ſunne gentle Eurus, whether thou wouldſt be called Subſolanus or Vulturnus rather, who art thought to blow the winds of a fauourable and ſmiling fortune, remoue thoſe inſolent blaſts of thine. For the hart intentiue to diuine things, and al enflamed with loue, heares and attends thee not.

Now come I then to thee, my [illegible] IESVS, tel me, goe to, what ſlumber, is this, which refreshed thy weary body with ſo gentle a shower of vapours? Thou being once tired in the heat of the day, ſateſt

ſateſt at the fountaine, attending the poore *Samaritan,* woman (b) with whom, as the antient *Iacob* with his *Rebecca,* thou ſtruckeſt a new contract of mariage. Again els-where being broken with toyle of trauelling sherwd iournyes, thou gotteſt to the mountaine tops about the shutting in of the day (c] to refresh thy wearied limmes with a short repoſe, when preſently hauing now hardly begun to enter into prayer, thou waſt faine abruptly to break it off. But what ſleepſt thou here now for. Nor doe I thinke thou art ſo drownd in ſleep, or ſo idle is to meditate on nothing: If thy loue deceiue me not, I should verily beleeue thou now reuolueſt in mind that ſacred mariage which thou one day waſt to contract with the Church, thy immaculate Spouſe, at that moſt happy tree of the Croſſe, when the

ſleep

sleep of death should bind thee both hand and foote, and from thine open side that other *Eue* should yssue forth, as once the forme *Eue* had done our common Parent, who sudenly arose, so built of the bone of *Adam*, cast into that prophetical and extatical sleep. (d) Or whether art thou not perhaps voluing and reuoluing many things within thee, studing and contriuing with thy self, what dowry to make thy new Spouse, and peraduenture thinkst vpon the ornaments and dressings for her head, earings, bracelets, carkanets, and wedding robes, al embrodred with the richest gemmes with such like nuptial honours, and presents fit for Spouses? Or thou designest, who knovves? the forme perhaps and solemne tables of Matrimony, vvhich hereafter in the publike Theatre of the vvorld; thou

art

art to celebrate vvith the Church and the holy Soule. It may be thou conſidereſt vvhat her pouerty is, and vvant of al things, and vvhat the reſt of al her goodly ſtock of miſeries; or vvherein only ſhe is richly furniſhed and abundantly vvel ſtored.

Or perhaps thou thinkeſt of yet more ful & happy things then theſe, which here thou dreameſt on, while thou ſleepeſt. For in thoſe gẽtle ſlumbers; thou takeſt in the humane hart, thou now plotteſt perhaps in mind, the immenſe glory thou wilt affoard the ſoule with a prodigal hand, who ſhal haue the grace to receiue thee courteouſly indeed. This doubtleſſe, thou handleſt, now volueſt, reſolueſt deſtineſt, and deſigneſt.

O great *Iacob*, while thou ſlept'ſt ſo, with thy head reſting on a hard ſtone, what ſtrange, what diuine things there didſt thou behold! And how many Angels were shewed thee on that ladder going vp and downe, so pitched on the earth and reaching vp to heauen. *Iacob* (as we haue in the sacred history) (e) flying the more then deadly hate & fury which his brother *Esau* bare vnto him, came to *Luza* where he made a stone his pillow, lying on the bare ground, in stead of a soft and easy bed, and behold he saw a ladder fixt on the ground extended to heauen, God leaning on the top thereof, and the Angels ascending and descending to and fro: when being astonished and amazed thereat, he cryed out. *The Lord is truly in this place, how terrible this place is!* And presently annointed it and set vp an Altar in the place and al hast gaue thanks to the Diuinity, and put the name of *Bethel* to it. O litle *Iacob*! O most louing IESV, rest in my hart a while (if it trouble

thee

thee not too much) though indeed it be but a hart lodging, and thou haſt but a ſtone for a pillow and bolſtre only, yet ſurely it wil be ſoft enough, as ſoone as thou ſhalt but powre theron the oyl of thy mercy. Let the hart then ſo daily conſecrated, be called *Bethel*, that is the houſe of God. The houſe of vanity! Ah neuer be it ſayd. But rather ſtrēgthen it my God, be ſure thou found it wel, leaſt the winds of inconſtancy and tempeſts ſhake it. But ſtand it rather immoueable as the rock of *Marpeia* in the midſt of the ſea daſhed with the waues & ſcornfully ſhaking them off.

(a) *Cant.* 5. (b) *Io.* 4 (c) *Luc.* 6. (d) *Gen.* 2. [e) *Gen.* 28.

MEDI-

XV. MEDITATION.

The preparatory Prayer.

Actiones nostras, &c.

THE PRELVDE.

A *Great storme was made in the Sea, so as the ship was euen couered ouer with waues; but he slept.* (a)

1. *Point.* Consider the nest where in the holy soule should liue and dye, is the thorny crowne of the most louing IESVS; for this sticks so deep into the crowne of the sacred head of the Spouse, as none may pul it off; and so is as safe being and a firme peace: and therefore wil I sing with the most holy *Iob: I wil dye in my nest, and like to the Palme wil multiply my dayes.* (b] And I wil alwayes cause, I say such a new increase of merits

merits in me, as there ſhal no day ſlip wherein I adde not ſome line or other to the abſolute pourtrait of vertue and ſanctity

2. *Point.* The bed wherein IESVS loues to reſt is the hart of pious men, and dedicated to his loue. If IESVS lodge but there, though he ſleep the while, al things goe wel and reſt quietly; and it were to no purpoſe to feare any winds, ſtormes, or thunders there. For the waues daſhing thereon doe but only foame and no more, againſt the rocks of *Epirus*; then breake in their retire and ſoone after come to nothing.

3. *Point.* IESVS reſting in the harts of Martyrs, makes them ſo generous and ſtout as they can equally endure the torments of fire, and water: and no meruail; for while IESVS takes but his reſt there, he giues them reſt.

So

So when we admit IESVS by receiuing the Sacrament of the Eucharist into the lodging chamber of our hart, there is nothing can trouble vs or disturb vs because IESVS is there who is our peace. (c)

(a) *Mat.* 18. (b) *Iob.* 39. [c) *Rom.* 16. *Ephes.* 2.

THE COLLOQVY.

SHal be directed, to the most sublime and diuine Sacramēt of the Eucharist: First extol its force and power, which at that time we feele in our selues. For the soule which receiues and retaynes IESVS in her house, how stout, how generous, how constant she becomes! Then inuite IESVS that he would often deigne to lodge in the Inne of thy hart, and there securly take his rest. But beware thou awakest him not in in his ſleep, nor euer ſuffer the noyſe of the world, and commotions of the mind to make any tumult there, or that any idle words (for the leaſt thing hinders) should diſturb his ſweet and gentle ſleepes.

Pater. Aue.

Sat eſt, IESV vulneraſti
Sat eſt, totum penetraſti
Sagittis ardentibus.

Procul procul hinc libido
Nam cæleſtis hic Cupido
Vincet ignes ignibus.

16

IESVS VVOVNDS AND PIERCED THE hart vvith the shafts of loue.

THE HYMNE.

THe Diuels Archer, Erbinger
Of lust blind Cupid did appear,
But durst not stay to bend his bow,
He saw the hart with arrowes glow,
Which made him slinke away the chast
And spotles hart he cannot blast,
Which being cleans'd from sinne, is shut
From that blind boy, whose only but
Are harts polluted, without white.
Behold the woũds Christ makes, delight
See where the Angels pointing stand,
Giue ayme, by lifting vp their hand;
Or rather while the shafts abound,
Wish they had harts that he might woũd.

THE INCENTIVE.

1. MY good Archer ſhoot, Ah ſhoot againe! ſhoot through this hart of mine, with a million of ſhafts, this refractory & rebellious hart to thy diuine loue: ſlay and kil al loue, which is not thine, or is aduerſary to it. O ſweet wounds! o deare to me! o arrowes dipt and tipt with hony.

2. And thou my hart, reuenge thoſe iniuries ſo ſweet, ſo acceptable, and for thy part alſo shoot thou againe into the hart of IESVS with a thouſand shafts, a thouſand pious loues, a thouſand bals of fiery loue.

3. The hart is neuer in ſo good plight as when it is transfixed with a thouſand points of sharpeſt loue and paine; ſo that the true loue of IESVS caſts but the flames where with I pyne, I burne with loue.

THE

THE PREAMBLE to the Meditation.

BVt what a Gods name doſt thou here, thou Pànder *Cupid*? Art thou ſo brazen faced as to preſume to abide where my loue IESVS is? Come hither you good Angels, thruſt forth this wicked brat of that *Cyprian* ſtrumpet, out of doores. Break his quiuer, ſnap his ſhafts a ſunder. For what a ſhameleſſe impudence is this and ſaucy boldnes, of that blind elf, that ſuch a cowardly Iack as he should not quake & tremble at the aſpect, yea euen but the ſhadow of my Lord IESVS, dreadful to heauen & earth? But, o powerful arrowes of thy bow my Chaſter *Cupid*! my delight! my IESVS! In the Northern ſeas they tel of a flowing Iland, which ſtands ſtil and as it were, caſts ankour as ſoon as shot into with burning ſhafts, enkindling fire as they fly. I beleeue it: For loe thy fiery ſhafts, very ſudenly ſtay and arreſt the ankored barke of my hart, ſayling in its ful courſe, and euen now moſt miſerably floating in the midſt of the ſea of the world. O loue I ſay not blind as he! For how directly ſhoots he at the marke, how dexterouſly and ready he diſcharges, & how powerful his ſhafts! Wherewith when *S. Auguſtine* was touched and wounded once he cryed out: (a) *Lord thou shotteſt into our hart, with thy charity, and thy Word we haue transfixed in our bowels.* But the time ſhal come, my doughty warriour, when from the diuine bow of thy humanity bent and ſtretched on the Croſſe; thou ſhalt ſhake and brandiſh ſeauen ſpeares of perfect victory, true ſymbols

ſymbols of the foyling, and vtter ruine of the enemy. For as the Prophet *Elizeus*. ſetting his hād to King *Ioas* his bow, bleſſed the arrow, with theſe words: *The shaft of ſaluation of the Lord and the shaft of ſaluation againſt Syria.* (b) ſo thy Diuinity ſuſteyning the humanity, impreſſed a certaine more diuine force into thoſe ſeauen laſt words of his wherewith like bow and arrowes they might trouble, diſſipat, and quite transfix the hellish legions. For there truly are thoſe shafts whereof once the royal Prophet ſung: *Thy arrowes are sharp, people shal fal before thee; into the harts of the Kings enemyes.* (c) O holſome blow! O happy chance! O admirable force of arrowes! For loe, the ſame both cure the crowned, & deeply wound thoſe who ſeeme in their opinion to be whole. Goe to then, be thou my hart the ſ. opeand bute , ſtand to it, why shrinkſt thou? ſtand I ſay , and ſtoutly take the shaft of loue into thee. Yea doe thou shoot too, retort , and wound againe. And be thou likwiſe as a heauenly bow: and doe thou ſtretch and ſtreyne thy ſelf with al thy nerues as much as thou canſt. Let thy ſighes and vowes shot like thunder-bolts and winged darts, freely mount vp the throne of God himſelfe. But firſt be they fired with thy heat; that they may fly the ſwiftter : adde alſo flames, begg'd and fetched from heauen, and as the moſt louing IESVS is al fire, al loue, ſo doe thou kindle fire, burne , loue , breake into ſighes, with frequent ſobs , which reaching vnto God may inſtantly reuerberate, and returne to thee againe, and draw forth bitter teares from thee in great abundance.

But

But thou, o incomprehensible loue, diuine spirit who so shadowest and sittest on the hart as heretofore in the first creation of things thou didst, when hatching the world from the rude, confused, and indigested Chaos thou conuerted, so that vast abysse of waters; (d] with the heauenly dew of thy graces, temper the flames of the boyling hart. For my hart like wax molt with the fire; with the sweet extasy of loue euen liquefyes with al, and so may I liquefy stil til I liquefy and melt away for altogether. Goe to then, with the finger of thy charity, expresse in me the liuely forme and image of thy loue, that after in my bowels I shal kindle, and take fire, and thou with water as it were shalt quench or temper the same, that there may be nothing found in me but diuine dewes, celestial flames.

Let this fire then burne and encreaſe in the midſt of waters ; and the fire of concupiſcēce being vtterly quenched , may theſe purer flames liue and eternally burne my hart , which neither the waters of tribulations , nor the roaring waues of temptations , nor any violence of ſicknes, nor the Scilla of calumniating tongues , nor the gulfs of blaſphemous mouths , nor laſtly the furious Charibdes of any puniſhments may euer extinguiſh it , for endles Ages.

(a) *Lib. 9. Conf.* c. 2. (b) 4.*Reg.* 13. (c) *Pſal.* 44. (d) *Gen.* 1.

XVI. MEDITATION.

The preparatory Prayer.

Actiones nostras, &c.

THE PRELVDE.

THou *hast wounded my hart, with thy loue* : ſayth, the beloued Spouſe to her Spouſe, in the burden or holding of her ſong. (a)

1. *Point.* Conſider the hart to be like to that Iland they ſay to be continually caryed and poſted here and there, with the waues of the northern ſea, nor euer to reſt til touched with burning ſhafts : ſo are mens harts being toſſed with the tempeſts of diuers concupiſcences, nor can be ſtaid or kept in, but touched and ſtruck with the dart of diuine loue. Hence that ſaying of *S.*

Augustine being once caryed away with the vogue and wind of euil affections and now ceasing from the course of his former impieties, *Thou hast shot our hart, my God, with thy charity.* (b)

2. *Point.* Consider the blessed felicity and happy state to be wished for of the hart, as wel wounded with the loue of IESVS as dying of the wound. For this is a kind of death whereof the Sonne of God himself and his holy Mother dyed; and which al pious soules are wont to dye of.

3. *Point.* Attend to what are the motions and exultations of the hart, touched with diuine loue. *Charity* (saith that great Coripheus of the Quier of I E S V S his louers] is patient benigne, not enuious, or seeking its priuate comodities.

(a) *Cant.* 4. (b) *Cant.* 4. (c) 2. *Cor.* 13.

THE

THE COLLOQVY.

SHal be directed to the Angels, beſeeching them to driue away *Cupid*, that infamous princock boy, that lewd ſtripling, to knap his arrowes aſunder, and to burſt his quiuer, that he may neuer more come neere my hart, or offer any violence to it.

En armatas flam̄is tendit̄
IESV manus, cor accendit
Hinc et illinc facibus
Age, totum comburatur
In favillam redigatur
Cor amoris ignibus

17

THE HART EN-FLAMED WITH THE LOVE of IESVS shines al vvith light and flames.

The Hymne.

Come Moyſes to the buſh, draw nere:
Now God Incarnate doth appeare,
Man's hart the buſh (ceaſe to admire)
With flames of loue he ſets on fire.
See here the ſcortching flakes and fume
Of prayer, which burne & not conſume,
But only droſſe of ſinne. Behold
A hart refin'd of tryed gold:
A Buſh wherin loue ſo contriues,
That IESVS, Phenix-like reuiues,
Amidſt ſweet aromatike ſents.
A buſh wherin one that contents
Is al in al. And now though rare
One bird in buſh is better fare.

THE INCENTIVE.

1. THe whole hart is al on fire these flames then either come from heauen; & deriue from IESVS, or al these fires are sprung from hel and lewd desires. Ah my litle soule! Why art thou so in doubt? Deliuer thy whole hart to IESVS, that he only may enflame it with the fires of diuine loue.

2. Behold his hands, feet, hart, eyes, face, the whole body: IESVS is nothing els but fire, naught but litle flames of loue, whatsoeuer he doth, speakes, suffers, breath but loue, and that the loue of thee.

3. O loue! o sweet loue! o flames of loue! Ah burne this hart I pray. Yea my soule, doe thou burne thee to ashes too in the loues of my IESVS; and in these sweet flames, may

may it liue, dye, reuiue againe, like another Phenix.

THE PREAMBLE to the Meditation.

IESVS was on the top of mount *Thabor*, in the friendly company of *S. Peter, Iames, Iohn, Moyses* & *Elias*; (a) when ſudenly his face began to ſhine like the ſunne, his garments to be as white as ſnow, and the hil itſelf to glitter ál with flashing rayes, flowing from his countenance. But when *Moyses* heretofore aſcended on mount *Sinay*, to receiue the law of God in ſtony tables (b) the people beheld al the place to be ſet on fire to ſparkle, to burne, to shine al ouer. Laſtly *Elias* chariot (c) the fiery ſword of the Cherubin, watching at the gate of Paradiſe, (d) the foure beaſts of *Ezechiel*, [e) and al furni-

furniture about them, seemed not onely to shine, but to burne also. But what said the Spouse of her beloued and his chast loue? *His lamp*, said she, *are lamps of fire and flames; many waters were not able to extinguish charity.* (f) O fires and liuing flames euen in the midst of flouds of waters! This is the fire which encloses the hart so, and sends forth such radiant and refulgent rayes, as banishing al darknes, al things shine and burne both within and without. Of this lamp mercy is the oyl; and that truly indeficient, as flowing from an inexhaustible chanel, the very bowels of God. This is that wal of fire, which God had prouised by the Prophet, (g) which being interposed; the lyons creast would fal, the enemy be forced to turne his back, and he be smit & strucke with a thunder-bolt, who should once goe about to set there

there to his sacrilegious hand. But of al these wonders, this is most to be wondred at, that as the greene bush amidst the purest flames did burne vntouched (h) and impeached a whit, and God himself was heard to preach therein, as in pulpit; so the hart encompassed al with flames, & therewith round beset, most constātly alwayes burnes and is not consumed, but euer shines and flasheth ligth, since IESVS raises and resuscitates those fires, and feedes the immortal flames. Marke here, how high the smoak of these fires mounts vp to heauen. Goe to then, come hither with your thuribles and incense: How nigh in a moment the incense of such fires sends forth most sweet odours to Heauen! How speedily the vowes and prayers commended to this fume, arriue at the throne of heauen! The Heauens with this exultaexhalation shal breath forth Nectar: The ayr repurged shal ſauour ſweetly, the threats and rage of Deuils shal expire; for indeed they can no more endure theſe odours, the grunting ſnowts of ſwine abide the breath exhaling from the ſweeteſt ſmelling lillyes; and therefore shal they be enforced to fly away, and returne againe into the inmoſt and moſt hidden receptacles of Hel.

This is the fire, this the flame, which quenches the heat of concupiſcence; for as one nayle driues out another, ſo the fire of diuine loue expels and repreſſeth the libidinous flames of baſe and carnal loues.

Burne therefore my hart, o *IESV*, the dearling of my ſoule, and let not the oile of the lamp be euer wanting: be this fire as a wal vnto me; (i) be it as a ſunne, and be this my chiefeſt ambition, that I burne and be conſumed

ſumed

ſumed with this flame: Yea, and be reduced into aſhes; then thoſe aſhes into a litle worme, and preſently become a new hart. O Metamorphoſis of loue! But firſt would I haue the old be throughly tryed, in the litle furnace of his loue, the droſſe, and al the dregs to be ſcoured thence, and no humane and terrene lees to be left behind, but meerly to take a heauenly ſtate vpon it: to liue a ſpiritual life, to feed on ſpiritual food to vſe a ſpiritual tongue, to haue ſpiritual feet and hands; yea diuine cogitations and affections, & not done by aſpects only, but euen Angelical. In ſumme may this hart, thus purged and purified, giue forth hereafter naught but a liuely and euerlaſting figure of a bleſſed immortality. So then doe thou my deareſt IESV) here fix thy hart, at laſt; dwel here in thy Palace; and here

here shoot forth the glittering rayes, of thy glory,

(a) *Mat.* 17. (b) *Exod.* 29. (c) 4. *Reg.* 2. (d) *Gen.* 3. (e) *Ezech.* 1. (f) *Cant.* 8. (g) *Zach.* 2. (h) *Exod.* 2. (i) *Zach.* 2.

XVII. MEDITATION.

The preparatory Prayer.

Actiones nostras quesumus, &c.

The Prelvde.

I *Came to send fire into the earth and what would I els but haue it burne.* (a)

1. *Point.* Consider how necessary it is the hart enflamed with loue, should mount vp and vanish into vapours; and so great is the force of this flame, as it ascends to heauen streight, where it arriues without impediment: nor hath the world, whit-

without God, ought that can ſatiate and replenish the boſome of the hart.

2. *Point.* Conſider, how ſubtle and actiue the flame of diuine loue is piercing, cleare, neuer idle, vnquiet, impatient to beheld shut vp in any other place then in the boſome of the Crucifix; where as in a furnace of loue, it purges and repurges ouer and ouer, and receiues new life and vigour againe.

3. *Point.* Note the matter and fuel of this fire to be al thoſe things which Superiours enioyne, in the execution whereof is manifeſtly diſcouered what force there is in this fire, (a] *Luc.* 12.

THE COLLOQVY.

SHal be directed to Christ whom I wil seeme to behold with two burning lamps in his hands: I wil beseech him, to purge whatsoeuer is vnperfect or vicious in me, and to reduce the very hart to dust & ashes: that a new may arise like a Phenix, which after he hath laid downe the spoyles or weedes of his mortallity, resuscitates a new, and reuiues againe from the tomb it-self, more beautiful and a great deale better.

Pater Aue.

O beata ſors amoris.
Poſt tot luſus, tot honoris
Signa, tot lætitiæ.

Diadema regni datur.
Et cor patris exornatur
Immortalis gloriæ.

18.

IESVS CROVVNES HIS DEARE HART WITH Palmes and Laurels.

THE HYMNE.

THe restles hart, which heretofore,
Could not stand stil, but euermore
Was beating oft with throbs opprest
Til now could neuer be at rest.
It was ambitious, now I find.
Naught could content th'aspiring mind:
Had honours, pleasures, wealth good store,
Yet euer craued, was seeking more:
Which shew'd there was yet somthing stil
Which this capacious hart might fil.
A triangle, the soule, hath three
Distinctiue powers. The Trinity
Is such, that fils it; rest is found,
Loe th'hart is quiet, new its crowned.

THE INCENTIVE.

1. YOu good Angels, weaue you garlands with garlands, laurels with laurels, and crowne therewith the fortunate hart, which then glories and triumphs most when with Olympian study; and labour of vertues and mortification it hath gayned but this prize, for reward, to deserue to be beloued of IESVS.

2. O ioyful! O festiual day! wherin we may behold and gather euen from thornes and toyles the purest roses; from sweat and armes, palmes and laurels; lastly of spitle, vinegre and clay immortal & eternal crownes: which IESVS, himself plants and fastens on with his owne hand.

3. What lookst thou then, o poore hart! and tremblest at the multitude

titude of euils, which enuirone thee and beset thee round. Cast thine eyes rather on the laurels which attend thee after thy victory. For nothing can breake or so much as moue him whom the hope and expectation of palmes erect susteynes.

THE PREAMBLE to the Meditation.

GOe to, you Angels, goe to, o blessed Spirits make hart with your palmes and laurels, from your posyes, weaue you garlands and with them deck you vp the triumphant hart, victorious now after so many assiduous labours, Crownes are sacred, free from thunder, priuiledged from the heauens, and signifye exemption and immunity. *Now the winter is passed away the showers blowne ouer and quite vanished* (a) Now

Now the lyonly rage of the ſworne and profeſſed enemyes of the hart is repreſſed, vanquiſhed,& tamed:prouide you eternal laurels, victorious palmes , and giue them into the hands of the moſt ſweet IESVS that he may ſettle on the hart , the crowns or garlands ſo prepared.

The magnanimous King *Dauid*, affecting much the fat and fruitful oliue ſymbol of mercy, humbly prayes (b] his hart, may be crownd with diuine mercies. The penitent *Magdalen* (c] and *Peter* (d) weeping bitterly, reſemble the Amaranth , an herb which in the midſt of waters retaynes both its natiue bitternes and perpetual greenes. The voluptuous, worldly , and licentious men, are wholy taken with roſes, and lyllies. *Let vs crowne our ſelues* ſay they, *with roſes , before they wither be there no meadow which our luxury rūnes not ouer.*

(e) O Phrigian luxury? O wantonnes! But now a dayes forsooth the Princes and Potentates of the earth, crowne not themselues so much with golden diadems and precious stones, as load them rather. O ambition! o pride! But what doth the most sweet IESVS, I pray! he loues the victorious palmes, with these crownes he decks his dearest hart. For they indeed haue truly merited those glorious wreaths who haue not only constantly opposed the hart as a target to receiue the shafts approaching of aduerse fortune, but euen as daring the enemy more slow to anger, haue scorn'd and derided dead it-self. Surely the squadrons of Martyrs, and Quiers of Virgins, triumphing in Heauen, cary Palmes in their hands: (f) howbeit the 24. Seniours ware on their heads crownes of gold (g) which through their

their glorious conqueſts and ſet triumphs by them made vpon their enemyes they had purchaſed to themſelues. *Bleſſe* therefore *the Lord* (h) thou holy ſoule, through whoſe ſingular and eſpecial fauour thou haſt atteined to the top of perfection *Praiſe thy Lord* (i) through whoſe mighty power, thou haſt walked and trampled on the ſands of the ſea, (k) croſſed the Iourdan with a dry foot, the people of harts incircumcized, and enemyes profeſſed, looking, on the while, and gazing with amazment: to whom ſo vanquiſhed, thou gaueſt lawes, and laidſt perpetual tributes on them, they being not able any wayes to barre thee paſſage into the land of promiſe and region of *Paleſtine*. Bleſſe thy God then o hart ful of Heauen, and al of fire. And ſince now thou haſt obteined a certaine pledge of felicity, an infallible hope, enter a Gods name at thy pleasure, with a notable and triumphant pomp into the Capitol of the heauenly *Hierusalem*; where so many purple Kings triũph as haue heretofore repressed their lewd concupiscences, and the insolence as wel of their interiour as exteriour senses.

Ioyne thee to the inuincible Martyrs, and keep among the Quiers of Virgins; let the body be thy triumphal chariot, which Saphirs and Carbuncles, most precious iewels embellish as with so many twinckling starres. Let Clarity, Agility, Subtility, Impassibility, those foure dotes of the blessed body, be as so many wheeles; and permit thy self to be drawne wheresoeuer the diuine spirit sitting on the coatch and wheeles shal snatch thee, or fly thou where thou wilt thy self, diuine loue

shal

ſhal play the Coach-man ? Beſides the Princes of darknes, ſigh and groane as they runne before the chariot whom thou haſt vanquiſhed with the ſingular demiſſion and lowlynes of mind. Let death it-ſelf be conſtreined likwiſe to put on the cheynes and follow after; ſince by the death of Chriſt thou haſt triumphed vpon it alſo, weakned and broken, and that already by the ſame guide and wagoner as before. Let the vanquiſhed world come in and make a part of the ſaid pomp; which then thou ſtoutly trampledſt vnder-feet; when with a generous ſcorne and loathing, contemning its wealth and honours, thou madſt no more reckoning of its vaſt immenſnes, inſolent cariages, and flanting promiſſes, then of a figure drawne in the water, or Chimæra laboriouſly framed in the foliſh ſhop of the phantasy. Draw I say these ancient cruel enemyes, now happily vanquished and tamed wel loaden with cheines and reproaches, before the oual and triumphant chariot, that is, the rich bootyes, noble spoyles, ample tropheyes and victories atcheiued in many warres. But especially haue care that sensuality aboue the rest, the chiefest part of the triumph, be tyed and bound to the Chariot, which with an heroical fortitude thou hast conquered, & made more like indeed to a dead then a liuing thing, pale, meagre and of so feeble forces as it may neuer after dare to appeare in the field, or make any resistance.

But now in warlike standards and enseignes, let the cityes and towers, which thou hast ouer-throwne, be painted; which kind, let the mad tower be first set downe, which thou had

had leueld with the ground, and let al the complices and confederates thereof, ſubdued and braught vnder-yoke, and ſo cheyned together be led, as ambition, vanity, arrogance, and the reſt of thoſe military troops. Let another banner exhibit the bloudy warres, to be read which thou haſt valiantly attẽpted, faught, and the victoryes nobly atchiued againſt luxury and rebellion of the ſenſes. Let thoſe gallant exploits be wouen here in ſilke, and waued in banners, vp and downe through the ayr as thou paſſeſt,; wherewith thou haſt maſtered and tamed thy fleſh, that fierce and cruel beaſt. Let the inuincible courage of thy mind be here ſeen and read, as faſts, abſtinences, auſterities, mortificatiõs, wherewith, as with a ſword and buckler, thou haſt fought againſt this fierce and miſcheuous enemy.

Let the Stygian *Pluto* alſo, that damned loue of riches, be caryed in an other flag; whom long ſince thou haſt trod vnder-foot, in preferring religious pouerty before al the treaſures of the world.

Let beſides the daſtard, weake, and languiſhing ſlouth, ſitting on her ſnayl, come forth in this triumph, which ſlow and ſluggiſh beaſt, thou haſt ſtirred vp with the ſharp prick of generoſity and diligence, and beyond al hope prouoked and preuayled with at laſt.

Laſtly in a table, higher then the reſt, let this inſcription be read, regiſtred in capital letters, for a record and perpetual memory.

THROVGH THE HELP, SVCCOVRS, AND MERITS OF THE MOST LOVING IESVS, HAVE WE FAVGHT, AND VANQVISHED AND ARE

ARE NOW CONVEYED TO HEAVEN, TO TRIVMPH THERE AMIDST THE GLORIOVS PALMES AND LAVRELS.

But now what remaines? forsooth this last of al; that when thou shalt consort thy self aboue, with those 24. Seniours, and Quiers of Angels; thou lay downe thy crowne at the feet of the immaculate Lamb, (l) chanting with those blessed Citizens of Heauen this oual and triumphing song: *Benediction & clarity, and thanksgiuing honour, vertue and fortitude, to our Lord for euer and euer.* Amen. (m)

(a) *Cant.* 2. [b) *Psal.* 102. [c) *Luc.* 7. (d) *Marc.* 26. (e) *Sap.* 2. [f) *Apoc.* 10. (g) *Apoc.* 4. (h) *Psal.* 102. (i) *Psal.* 147. (k) *Exod.* 14. *Iosue.* 3. (l) *Apoc.* 4. (m) *Apoc.* 7.

XVIII. MEDITATION.

The preparatory Prayer.

Actiones nostras, &c.

FIRST POINT.

I Wil fayne my ſelf to be armed at the top of the Hil, whither I had got with great endeauour,and much labour and trouble. I wil caſt and reflect the eyes of my mind on the diuers wayes and traces I had paſſed thither; the precipices I eſcaped, and the perils of aſſaſſinates and wild beaſts I haue auoyded: For ſo it is indeed with ſuch as haue attayned to the top of perfection. For theſe ſhould attentiuely conſider with thẽ-ſelues as from an eminent place,how many and how great dangers, temptations, and ſiniſter chances, being aſſi-

assisted by the diuine mercy, they haue escaped from the world, and al the rest of the enemies of mans saluation.

2. *Point.* I wil consider the lawes of these lifts to be such, that. *None shal be crowned but who haue lawfully faught & contẽded therein* (a) *The Palme belongs but to the Conquerour*: (b) and I wil admire also the goodnes of God, for crowning vs himself with his graces, and commanding the Angels to crowne vs with those laurels, which we haue purchased to our selues with our owne vertues.

3. *Point.* I wil ponder and weigh with my self, with what riuers of ioyes the hart flowes, to whom is affoarded to arriue to the top of diuine loue, and who already beholds his owne perseuerance; which only vertue makes vs blessed and secure, without which the rest auayle but litle

litle, or nothing, for perseuerance alone is it, which is crowned.

(a) 2. *Tim.* 2. *Apoc.* 7.

THE COLLOQVY.

SHal be directed to the most louing IESVS, to whom of duty al our crowns belong. For we are not conquerours so much as vanquished, while he indeed hath broken and subdued our refractory and rebellious hart. Wherefore to him as to a most mightie conquerour, and victorious Captain, with those 24. Seniours in the Apocalips (a) are we to offer vp our crownes, palmes, laurels, with this solemne verse of theirs; *Benediction and clarity, and thancks giuing, honour and vertue, and fortitude for euer and euer be to IESVS the Conquerour and triumpher to come.* Amen.

(a) *Apoc.* 4. & 7. Pater. Aue.

IESVS CELEBRATES THE HEAVENLY Nuptials in the hart.

THE HYMNE.

THe nuptial supper, now I see,
O happy soule! prepar'd for thee;
The table's couerd: but what seat,
Hast thou for thy repose? What meat?
Except a Lamb, I nothing find,
The amourous Spouse is now so kind,
That what he fed thee with before;
From th'eye shalbe conceal'd no more.
As with a fleece, in Species white,
He long on earth appear'd in sight.
As with a fleece, by grace gaue heat:
But now behold the Lamb thy meat.
In him repose, freed from annoy
By seeing, comprehend, enioy.

THE INCENTIVE.

1. IESVS the bloudy Spouſe or Spouſe of bloud [a] leads his beloued, whom now long ſince he purchaſed with the price of his life, vnto the Nuptial ſupper of the Lamb, into the heauenly Bride-chāber. The hart therefore (who admires not] is the banqueting roome of theſe Nuptials and the Bed-chamber of the Spouſe IESVS himſelf.

2. It is a ſupper truly, becauſe theſe ioyes are not affoarded til after the toyles of the day and labours paſt. Expect not lampes; here hanging on ſumptuous and precious ſeelings: Theſe Pallaces ſhine within, and without ſunne, moone, and ſtarres. *The Lamb himſelf is the lamp within,* (b) and he the banquet Hoſt, and Gheſt who is the Spouſe.

3. Seeſt

3. Seest thou this royal Table here These things are al prepared for thee: Seekest thou daintyes? Hardly are thy seen of mortal eyes. Such as sit downe here are alwayes feeding, they drinke without gluttony, are alwayes satiated, and yet a-thirst, without any loathing or irksomnes at al. Behold al things are ready. *Come to the wedding, the Spouse cals.* (c)

(a) *Exod.* 4. (b) *Apoc.* 21. (c) *Mat.* 22.

THE PREAMBLE to the Meditation.

IESVS, receiues the soule, whom he gratiously beheld, though fowly dight with her immundityes before, and now hauing cleansed her with purging waters, and adorned (a) with feminine brauery, takes her I say, not only to his Spouse, (b)

(b) but if ſhe keep her holily and
chaſtly to him, caſting her out of the
moſt miſerable banishment of this
life, he leades her vnto the great ſo-
lemnity of the Nuptials, into the
heauenly houſe of his Father: where
he tyes her eternally to him with an
indiſſoluble knot of wedlock. Whereto belongs that ſacred Epithala-
mium: *Let vs reioyce and exult; and
giue glory to him; becauſe the Nuptials
of the lamb are come, and his Spouſe hath
made herſelf ready, and she hath had
giuen her shining and white ſilke to we-
are.* (c) Yt is ſurely a great matter
to be reckoned of the family of the
King of Kings, more to be accoun-
ted among his freinds and familiars;
but moſt of al to beheld the Sonne
of God, the brother and coheyr of
Chriſt: I wil ſpeake more boldly
yet; this ſame is ſurely more honou-
rable then al theſe to be called in

the weding the Spouſe or Wife of the Lamb, that is, partaker in a manner of his bed and bord, companion of his throne & crowne. And this is that honour if I be not deceiued, which the Prophet Eſay meanes: (d) *I wil giue then a place in my houſe, and within my wals; and a better name then ſonns and daughters.* For children being but a ſlender part or portion of parents, chalenge and retayne indeed much of their right and ſubſtance from them: but for man and wife, ſo great is the ſociety and community between them of their whole life & of al their goods and titles, and they are bound together with ſo ſtreight a tye, as how farre ſo euer they be aſunder, yet are held to be as is were in one place, and al one, which happens alſo in the celeſtial wedlock of IESVS with the ſoule. *For who adheares to God is in al one ſpirit with him,*

as

as the Apoſtle (e) hath taught. Whence it is, that the ſoule perfectly vnited with God, is not only diuine. but in a certaine manner (if I may ſo ſay) is made God. And hence is al (whatſoeuer it is, which is ſurely very great) that dignity; profit, and ſweetnes of theſe nuptials. For looke whatſoeuer els beſides haue any connexion with them, doe al euen flow from thence, as from an endleſſe ſpring of al good and beatitudes; eſpecially thoſe three, (to ſay nothing of thoſe of the body] to wit, the moſt ſingular and eminent dotes of the ſoule eſpouſed & wedded to IESVS, as Viſion, Comprehenſion, Fruition: (f) Which are not procured her either of parents or nature it-ſelf, but being ſo poore a Spouſe, are moſt bountifully affoarded her by IESVS the Spouſe himſelf (as with Kings is wont when they match with any of of low degree, most richly to endow their beloued Spouses, by reason of their nuptials had between them. But in reguard these things of themselues are greater then can be worthily weighed by vs, much lesse expressed, the diuine Scriptures, doe lightly shadow at least and adumbrate in a sort al the excellencies and delicious fruits thereof, with the pleasant and most apt figure (for our capacity) of royal nuptials, and a wedding supper. (g) The reason is, for that no noises of affaires & negotiations, nor cares, which commonly fal out by day, doe not trouble or disturb the peace and delights of suppers; & for the feasts of royal Nuptials, they vse especially to be very curious and dainty indeed, where no part of the senses abounds not with exquisite delights. Here the eyes are fed with various Emblems of the tapistries of the

the Hal most gallant to behold, with the gorgeous apparel of the Ghests and waiters also, with the gold of the plates, and iewels of the whole furniture there. Here the eares are charmed with the artificious harmony of musical instruments & voyces. Here the sent most sweetly is perfumed with the delicate odours of flowers and herbs, and boxes ful of the sweetest oyntmēts: the palat seasoned & relished with delicious wines, and the daintyest viands; purchased with the greatest study and industry; and sought for farre and neere by al the exquisit meanes that may be deuised, and dressed especially by the rarest Cookes. Lastly, to the end the sense of feeling, the most brutish sense of al the rest, might not want it's peculiar delights also, the touching hath its proper delectation, from the softnes of downy beds, and

curious

curious carpets, from the feathers, and downe of swans and the like. Let vs runne ouer a while, if you please, the gardens & pictures of the great *Assuerus*, that from that feast, the royallest perhaps that euer was in the memory of men, by ghesse at least we may gather in some manner, what a bãquet it is, which IESVS furnisheth forth in the hart of his Spouse.

He then, as wel, to shew the riches of the glory of his Kingdome, and the greatnes and the ostentation of his power; as also in the third yeare of his raigne, to celebrate publikely the day wherein first he tooke a perfect possession of Susa the chiefe seat of his Kingdome, prepared a *Persian*, royal, and a sumptuous banquet. For first *Assuerus* himself was the Master of the feast and who was he? He raigned from *India* to *Ethiopea*, from the East to the

the West: and what more? He gaue lawes to 127. Prouinces, appointing so many Prefects and Gouernours to them, who in the Kings name might administer iustice. *Assuerus* therefore was a mighty and most puissant King; yea truly he had conquered and subdued to his owne dominion the whole world, if we beleeue but his owne Epistle: (i) though indeed I should thinke it rather to be no more then a meere exaggeration of insolent men, who extending their bounds a litle wider, vse to flatter themselues with the Empire streight of the whole world: But be it so as they boast of & make their braggs, Assuerus yet shal seem but a fly compared with God himself; nor euer shal though he puffe vp himself neuer so much, ariue to the bulke and worth of an Elephant. IESVS, the Master of this feast,

not

not only as God, but euen also as man, is the Soueraigne & supreame Lord of al things, in whose loynes is written King of Kings, and Lord of Lords, (k) and at whose aspect & tribunal comming to iudgement shal *Assuerus* himself appeare one day, yea tremble and groane the while. The rest may likewise be gathered by this: Yet if you please let vs suruay them more perticularly that our purpose & scope may appeare more clearly.

Susa was not the head-Citty of the kindome of *Persia*, but a pleasant and most delicious *Tempe*, which that riuer *Coaspes* washed as it went a long; whose waters Kings, and those very farre remote from thence, made vse of for daintyest drink: and for the amenity of the place; it tooke the name of Lilly, which *Susa* signifies in *Persia*. Here therofore they reposed

reposed and lodged themselues, and that truly in those royal and princely gardens, wodds and groues [1) in the Spring especially as we may beleeue. Here not only the pleasant variety of flowers and herbs made a wanton daliance but euen of the beautifullest trees also; in disposing whereof in checker-wise, and distributing the allyes, walks, and arbours the royal hands themselues, after the Countrey fashion, had labowred to some purpose. But what trow you was the rest of the garnishment of this festiual Court Where the Pauilions were of a costly and rich stuffe; of cerulean, ætherean, and of the colour of the Hyacinth, whose curteynes hung with strings of purple silk, fastne with ringes made of iuory: at either end these rich and stately Canopyes were gallantly susteyned with marble

ble pillars; beneath lay humble pallots on the ground a pleasant pauement, to rest vpon al of gold and siluer, streyed with the fayrest mantles and rich carpets (as the 70. Interpretours signify) wrought al ouer, embrodered and curiously set forth with needle-works of roses, and diuerse other flowers, glittering and beguiling the senses : besides al which, the pauement it-self shined al of a certaine square stone, and that in quadruple wise ; enterstinguished with in the emerald, and touch-stone, and (as the Hebrew hath) with marble and Hyacinth being certaine titles forsooth, diuersifyed al in an admirable manner.

And these for the most part were prepared for the common Ghests; for I should thinke those of the better sort, were al entertained in the immost lodgings of those Princely

Pa-

Palaces, where with tapiſtryes and pictures, were al the roomes and lobbeyes ſumpteouſly hāg'd. Could there be euer any thing either for maieſtie more royal and magnificent or for luxury and delight more ſoft and delicious? O childish toyes, & meerly gugawes! O looſe cogitations, of the ſoule, euen bending to the earth! why creepeſt thou on the earth, thou litle muſh rump, and pleaſeſt thy ſelf ſo much with theſe trifles? Meaſure with the eyes of thy mind at leaſt, the vaſt immenſnes of the Heauens gaze if thou canſt, and behold the ſunne, moone, and the reſt more then common people of that ſtarry houſe; which are but onely outward ornaments: for thoſe within, farre different from them, tranſcending not only the faculty of the ſenſes, but euen the agility of the mind also are meerely laid out of sight. Heare the mellifluous Bernard: (m) *That same indeed is the true and onely ioy, which is not of the creature, but is truly conceiued of the Creatour himself, and which being possessed by thee no man can take away from thee: where to compared al pleasure otherwise is but sorrow, al sweetes but bitternes, al beautie deformity. Lastly al other things nought els but tedious and irksome, which otherwise might seeme more pleasing and delightful.*

Now then, which is the other point; looke we into the great *Assuerus.* Ghests [n] and directours of the feast. Of these I note two sorts, some purple Heroes of tke *Persians* and chiefe Prefects of those Countreyes and Prouinces 127. in nomber; who al (leauing magistrates of inferiours orders behind them in their roomes, to take vp differences

accur-

accurring the while) flock to thy City & Princely Court, to that great feaſt : the other Gheſts were the common ſort of the City of *Suſa* itſelf, from the higheſt to the loweſt a vaſt people vvithout head or certaine number of them.

But for the miniſters and vvaiters there, I ſeeme alſo to behold tvvo orders of them ſome Prefects of the royal Palace ; vvho as Stervvards, Vſhers, and Sevvers of the feaſt appointed and placed the Gheſts, preſcribing lavves and rules to them to be kept amongſt them ; others to execute leſſer and inferiour offices, as Butlers, Taſters, Cup-brearers, and the reſt of vvayters al : But if compared vvith the Angels, as vvel the Pages, and others of that diuine table ; as the bidden Gheſts themſelues, or either vvith the number or ſplendour, of the reſt of the bleſſed

Citizens of heauen , thoſe are but dvvarſs ; theſe Giants, thoſe vvretches, and for manners moſt cõmonly vvicked, theſe bleſſed and happy; yea moſt holy theſe except a fevv, an ignoble and baſe people , and theſe not only moſt graue Senatours , but Kings and Monarks al vvithout exception.

Behold here the Queene-Mother of God (to amit the Spouſe himſelfe , behold , the Patriarks , Prophets, Apoſtles, Martyrs, Confeſſours , Virgins , and al the reſt of the Court of Heauen , and let the Medes and Perſian Gheſts alone. Yet ſtil *Aſſuerus* (o) vants & Boaſts of the bowels & diſhes of his feaſt. Be it ſo, let vs ſet downe thẽ to eate & drink our fil, for this is the ſumme of al.

The diſhes, plates, and trenchers, are often changed ; ſuch is the multitude and variety there, and ſtore of

ſiluer

ſiluer gold, and other precious veſſels: For here they eat and drinke alſo in gold, and cups made al of gémes. As for the cups the Septuaginta auerre there was one made of Carbuncles, ſurely of a vaſt and immenſe price, to wit, of thirty thouſant talents, which of our florens comes to more then 101. millions. Let no man after this ſpeake or wonder any more at the ſuppers, exceſſe, coſts of *Cleopàtra*, *Lucullus*, or *Heliogabalus*. But what was the meate now brought to the table? The ſacred Scriptures ſpeake not a word thereof for that perhaps al might gueſſe then, if they would, as wel by the *Perſian* pomp, very vſual in thoſe things, and now brought into a prouerb, as by the great oſtentation touched aboue of the plates, cups, and diſhes had in that feaſt. What the drinke? Forſooth the best sorts, as became the royal magnificence: there was aboundance of al and the choycest (p) wines that could possibly be had, but on that condition that none should be compelled to drinke more or lesse; but euery-one haue liberty to drink as much and as litle, as he would. Surely a holsome and laudable law of the King. For this tyrannical order of *Let him doe reason or begone*, sprũg first no doubt from the Greek Tauernes, of I know non what *Caldus*, *Biberius*, or *Mero* (q) But now goe to, thou great admirer of the *Persian* banquet: vvhat account makest thou of the gold, siluer, ievvels, in those cups and dishes? This gold, siluer, ievvels, beleeue me are but a harder kind of earth, vvhereto the sunne & starres haue giuen a colour and some lustre; vvhereon I say, lest auarice perhaps might set to great a price, nature had vvissel hid them in the vvomb or bovvels of the elements, and these also vvhere they are most in vse, and vvorne of al, become but cheap, and of litle worth. But for meats and drinks what they are, appeareth then, when hardly being let downe into the stomake they are streight egested thence. And wilt thou compare this filth, this dirt [to say no worse) with the riches, and delights of heauen, with the Nuptials of IESVS with the Euangelical supper, with the vision of the diuine Essence, lastly with those delights and inexhaustible pleasures, which flow incessantly from that ocean of the highest good? The great *Iohn* saw (r) this table in his Apocalyps, and wondered at it; the royal *Psalmist* saw it likwise, and wholy astonished, exclaymed: *They shal be inebriated with the plenty of thy house, and thou shalt make them drink of the torrent of pleasure.* (s) But take here a litle this simple tast therof. *Al the goods of this world are nothing els, but as rinds and springs of the fruits of Paradise, cut off: and if the rinds and springs be such that men euen raie with the loue and desire of them, what shal the fruits themselues be, and the apples of Paradise it-self? and if such be the fruits and apples; what shal the rest be of those more solid and better meats? Surely they shal be such as they may alwayes be eaten without loathing, and alwayes desired without anxietie.* (t)

And now finally how long haue these feasts of *Assuerus* lasted? A hundred & eightye dayes at most; scarce half a yeare, especially if we speake of the feasts of the Peeres and Nobles; for the cōmon sort, continued hardly a weeke in these transitory delightes.

Take

Take me here a hundred thousand yeares, yea a thousand millions of yeares of this Nuptial supper, which IESVS furnisheth in the louers hart, and you shal find no end of the feast, which end yet, if you seeke further, measure Eternity. As long as Heauen and God shal be, these Nuptials shal continue alwayes. Not so, in this banquet of *Susa*. For (oh inconstancy of humane things!) behold how in the tables of Assuerus himself *mourning occupies the last of ioyes.* (u) After the *Persian* King had wel carroused, & now al enflamed with *Bacchus*, deep in his cups, & thought he had done but litle yet, if he shewed not the Queene *Vasthi*, to his Ghests; because she, either of pride or modesty rather, refused to come into the drunken presence of al those Princes, by the King her husbād, she was fowly & ignominiously in-

intreated, in the very banqueting roome it-ſelf, weere ſhe feaſted with her Ladyes, being thruſt from the royal throne and dignity, was refuſed and reiected by him. Goe to now, and praiſe the feaſts and nuptials of the great *Aſſuerus*, if you wil; or rather be wiſe and admire, and loue the celeſtial Nuptials of the Lamb.

(a) *Ezech.* 16. (b) *Oſee.* 2. (c) *Apoc.* 19. (d) *Iſa.* 56. (e) 1. *Cor.* 6. (f) *S. Tho.* 1. 2. q. 4. ar. 3. (g) *Luc.* 14. *Mar.* 22. (h) *Eſter.* 1. (i) *Eſter.* 13. (k) *Apoc.* 19. [l] *Eſter.* 1. (m) *Bern. ep.* 114. (n) *Eſter.* 1. (o) *Eſter.* 1. (p) *ibid.* (q) *Cicero. lib.* 5. *Tuſcul.* (r) *Apoc.* 6. & 21. (ſ) *Pſal.* 55. (t) *Bellarm. de fel. SS.* (u) *Pro.* 14.

XIX. MEDITATION.

The preparatory Prayer.

Actiones nostras quesumus, &c.

THE PRELVDE.

B*Lessed are they who are cald to the Nuptial supper of the Lamb.*

1. *Point.* Cōsider the higheſt dignity (then which a greater cānot be imagined) as wel of the ſoule, in loue which IESVS, which from an abiect and baſe condition is aduanced to the Nuptials of God himſelf, as of the humane hart, wherein theſe diuine Nuptials are celebrated. W*hence comes it, O humane ſoule,* ſaith S. Bernard, (a] *whence happens this ſo ineſtimable glory to thee, that thou shouldeſt deſerue to be his Spouſe, on whom the Angels wish to gaze? How happens this,*

that

that he shouldbe thy Spouse, whose beauty the sunne and moone admire, at whose beck are al things changed? What wilt thou yeald to thy Lord for al he hath thus afforded thee, to be his companion at table, and compartener of his Kingdome; lastly his bed-fellow, and to haue the King himself to lead thee into his chamber? And by and by behold with what armes of mutual charity, he is to be embraced, and loued againe, who hath made such reckning of thee; and at last: forget thy people, and thy fathers house: Forsake carnal affects, vnlearne secular mãners, absteine from former vices, commit al naughtie customes to obliuion.

2. *Point.* Weigh how great, sincere, and solid, the pleasures, are like to be, which the Spouse prepares for thee in the Nuptial supper: suruey al things which vnder heauen, are precious delight ful, and

deare

deare to men, in the ayr, earth, or ocean Sea, and then reason with S. Augustine thus: *If, my Lord, thou affordest so much to vs in prison; what wilt thou doe in the Palace? For since here al things are so exceeding good and delectable, which thou hast conferred on the euil aswel as the good; what wil those be which thou hast laid vp for the good onely? If so various and innumerable thy guifts are, which now thou equally distributest to frends and enemyes, how great and innumerabbe, how sweet and delectable shal they be, thou wilt bestow on thy freinds only! If in this day of teares and mourning, thou impartst such things what wilt thou doe on the nuptial day?* Hearest thou this my soule, and yet exclaymest not? *Blessed be he who shal eate bread in the Kingdom of God.* (b)

3. *Point.* Attend to this also; how of the ten Virgins of the Ghospel (c] being al Virgins indeed, that is,

Virgins of the Gospel

is, eſpouſed to Chriſt through true and ſincere faith, and who had ſometimes pleaſed the Spouſe in carying lamps of good works in their hands, fiue were become fooliſh, and from the nuptials and wedding ſupper oh hard fortune! quite excluded. Beware thou be not of their number let thy lamp be alwayes burning, and ſending forth light; let the oyle of charity abound in thy lamp, and euen, flow ouer, and eſpecially take heed thou neuer ſleep or ſlumber a whit, nor be ſurprized vnaware, ſuſpecting nothing of death, or iudgement, or be vnprouided. Haue continually ringing in thine eares, that voyce of thy Spouſe *Vigilate*, ſo often whiſpered in thy hart, that when that cry ſhalbe heard *Behold the Spouſe comes, goe forth and meet him*, thou maidſt preſently meet him chearfully comming to thee,

and

and with him enter into the wedding. For woe and a thouſand woes to them, who vnmindful wholy of ſo great a good, and deafe to the words of God, being taken napping drown'd in ſleep with their lamps extinguiſhed, and ſo excluded from the ſweeteſt nuptials of the lamb, ſhal be forced to cry out in vayne, *Lord, Lord open to vs*; on whom that iron bolt ſhal be obtruded, *I know you not*, or that wholy as lamentable; *The gate is shut.*

[a) *Bern. ſer. 2. de mut. aquæ in vinum.* [b) *Luc.* 14. (c) *Mat.* 25.

THE COLLOQVY.

SHal be directed to IESVS the Spouſe. Eſpecially thou ſhalt yeald him thankes with al thy powers, for chooſing thy ſoule to be his Spouſe, for louing it ſo dea-

rely

rely hitherto, and endowing it with the espousal guifts. Then shalt thou humbly beseech pardone of him, for hauing so coldly answered to his feruent loue, wherewith he hath so often preuented thee; and sometimes perhaps for breaking thy faith to him so firmly engaged. Lastly by that his loue; wherewith he hath so of ten preuented thee, shalt thou most earnestly beg at his hands, that through his grace thou maist be continually vigilant, and prouided for that last Adüent, which is like to be at mid-nigh, when perhaps thou least suspectest the same; that then thou maist meet him, with thy burning lamp, and with the prudent Virgins enioy him and his nuptial feast for euer. (a)

(a) *Mat.* 25.

Pater. Aue.

IESVS MANIFESTES HIMSELF AND THE MOST holy Trinity in the mirrour of the hart.

THE HYMNE.

THe Painter cannot draw a face,
T'expreſſ to life each feature, grace,
And figure, with proportion fit
Except the partie drowne doth ſit:
But heer in th'hart by being ſeen,
God drawes the picture which had been
Before imperfect: though't were neat,
And often toucht, 'twas not compleat.
Til now, it lightned as vpon ſee,
True picture of the Trinity.
The colours ſtem'd did fak and eye,
But now shal laſt eternally.
While heer the hart doth quiet ſit,
By viſion God doth figure it.

THE INCENTIVE.

1. THe hart which loues God truly and perfectly indeed, is a heauenly Paradise; so flowers it ouer and swimmes in delights; not the counterfeit, and transitory delights of this world, but of the other life; such as here, neither eye hath seen, nor eare hath heard, nor hath ascended into mans hart (a)

2. Here now IESVS stands not behind the wal, peeping at this Spouse through a grate; (b) but, which she beg'd at his hands, shewes her his face, the diuine Essence, the three diuine Persons, so cleerly and manifestly indeed, as euen the images themselues expressed, reflect againe in the Chrystal of the hart. O Paradise! O delights! O ioyes!

3. The hart faints through aboundance

dance of loue and delights; and nigh bursts with al, O man! what a beast thou art, if hearing of these pleasures, thou rather choosest the husks of swine? How like a block and stone, if yet thou louest not IESVS?

[a] *Rom.* 8. (b) *Cant.* 2.

THE PREAMBLE to the Meditation.

SO great is the future beatitude to the soule which loues IESVS dearely indeed, that mortal men being drowned in sensuality & mire, cannot easily conceiue it in the mind, nor lesse (without diuine light and hope) expect it. For (which S. Paul (a) took out of the prophecy of Esay. (b) *The eye hath not seen, nor eare heard, nor hath it ascended into the hart of man, what God hath prepared for such as loue him.* Surely those two most

wise

wiſe and worthy men, to the end they might clearely propoſe the greatenes and amplitude of the heauenly beatitude, aſſumed the firſt kind of meaſure to wit the ſpacious orbs of eyes, ſeeming moſt capacious, which though ſhut in a litle corner as it were, yet now and then get forth, wander & expatiate farre and wide, not only, into the vaſt champian fields, huge mountayne tops, and the golden and gemmy bowels of the waters, but with help eſpecially of Mathematike inſtruments reach euen to the very heauens themſelues, wel nigh of an infinit diſtance from vs, and therein diſcouer the lighteſt ſpots, changes, and errours. And yet this ſcantling is found to be leſſe then ſo to conclude or comprehend beatitude. *The eye hath not ſeen.*

Wherefore with the eyes ſince we only

only apprehend things present, but with hearing moreouer as by histories perceiue those thīgs which haue been formerly acted, or now are wrought in any other place, or shal hereafter come to passe, the eares haue seemed more apt to measure the thing proposed. But so neither, the immensnes of beatitude could be contained. *Nor the eare hath heard.* There remained now the vessel, for bulk surely not great, yet for capacity indeed most ample, *the hart of man.* For in the shop of the hart we frame, cherish, and embrace, as our proper issues, not only what our selues haue seen, with our eyes, or heard by relation from others but euen many other things also, which can not truly exist at al, as golden mountaines, Chimeras, Hippocentaures, and the like: And yet so neither, *hath it ascended into the hart of man,*

what

what God hath prepared for ſuch as loue him. This thing according to S. Auguſtin. *Is not comprehended through charity, it tra̅ſcends al vowes & wishes.* Shal we therefore diſpaire? *No it cannot be eſteemed, it may be yet purchaſed* Goe to yet let vs value it, howſoeuer, and as wel as beating the price, let vs cheapen it as we can. I for my part am truly of this opinion, that we are much taken and caried away with nothing more then with pleaſure, nor doe I miſlike them who are ſo, if they be ſolid, ſincere and honeſt pleaſures we hung ſo after. But beleeue me there can be nothing more ſweet and delicious, then the ioyes and iubelies of the hart, drowned in the loue of IESVS, and wherein IESVS deliciats himſelf? For why? It is a Paradiſe truly and not that terreſtrial one (though for the amenity of the ſoyle and ayr, and the exceeding plenty of flowers, trees, and fruits, it were so glorious and the very name of Paradise it-self imports no lesse then a place of pleasures and delights] but is indeed a heauenly Paradise into the allyes whereof and first walks, *S. Paul* being hardly admitted, was so lulled with al delights, that forgetting himself and al things else besides he was able to tel no more then this, *I know a man*; saith he, *whether in body I know not, or without the body I know not God knowes, to be rauished into the third heauen, and to haue heard so mysterious words, as man might not vtter.* (c) But what were they whence so great a feeling of pleasure, and delight results? Touch we the thing it-self, with the needly of faith only. In that celestial Paradise of the blessed hart, IESVS laying his Pilgrime habit a side, and the

the vayle of faith wherewith he was shrowded, shal exhibit his humanity to be ſeen and enioyed face to face: I haue ſaid too litle, yea his diuine eſſence alſo. This perhaps were enough to beatitude yet wil he cauſe the three diuine Perſons, Father, Sonne, and Holy-Ghoſt. to be ſo preſent, as they may not only be ſeen, but euen ſeeme in a manner to be touched alſo.

Beſides, in this natiue and moſt lucid mirrour of al things, many other things, nigh infinit for nomber, for beauty and variety ſurely admirable, ſhal ſhine with al, with ſo new alwayes & ſo fresh an obiect, that as long as eternity ſhal laſt they ſhal not breed any tedious ſnes in the beholders, or euer diminish the thirſt of ſeeing and beholding more, Here therefore, as in a liuely picture expreſſed in their colours, thoſe mysteries of faith and religion shal be truly represented, which now hardly are but shadowed, and with al our endeauour neuer wholy atteined. The Incarnation of the Word in the Virgin, the Oeconomy of mans Redemption, the diuine prouidence in administring things, the admirable and most hidden reasons of punishing the good and prospering the wicked: lastly, the lawes, traces, and rapts of diuine loue, by which he hath at last conducted the hart which loues him; sweetly indeed and yet strongly, now by the pleasant, and then the horrid paths, now of ioy then of sadnes, into the seats of al beatitudes From the cleere knowledge of al which verities, especially the obiect of the diuine Nature, and Persons, and conceiuing the images in the mind, of so excellent and admirable things, who sees not

not very soueraigne and nigh incredible ioyes to arise?

Queene *Saba*, scarce entring into the roome where *Salomon*, was fel into so great admiration, and was so rapt and transported with delight, at the order pompe, magnificence, especially at the presence of the King himself, that recouering breath at last, which she had nigh lost, she cryed out aloud: *Blessed are thy men, & blessed thy seruants who stand alwayes before thee, and hearken to thy wisdome.* (d) Yet these are but toyes, chips, trifles, compared with the presence and sight of God.

They report of S. Francis, that being once sadder then ordinary, he was so taken and rauished with the short modulation an Angel made with the lightest touch of his thumb on a Harpe, as he seemed to himself to be no more on the earth, but to be conuersant in heauen, amid the blessed Spirits there. (e) Good God! If these (which in heauenly delights is likely one of the least amongst them) so short and slight touches of the Angelical hand, as they could hardly be heard, were yet able to rauish the holy man, what would the harmony worke of so many Angelical and humane voyces, what exultatiōs would be there what dances and iubelyes? Besides, if the meanest things in heauen, as songs and dances, so delight and tickle harts, what wil the rest doe, both for number and dignity farre greater? What is more poore and slender with vs thē a bare & simple thought of God? Yet *Dauid* in his greatest troubles and afflictiōs when he felt himself most opprest, with the tip of the lips only of his soule, as it were, would lick in this celestial &

diuine

diuine hony, and therewith take extreame pleaſure. *I was mindful of God,* ſaith he, *and took delight.* (f)

Againe hauing but a thought only the fruition of God, of meere ioy he could hardly containe himſelf; but ſing in triumph. *I haue reioyced in the things which haue been told me we shal goe into the houſe of the Lord.* (g) Which triumphal verſe of the Royal Pſalmiſt, when our Angelical Bleſſed Aloyſius, being neere his death through weakenes, could not wholy bring forth, *Reioycing* ſaith he, *we goe reioycing*, and with that ſo broken and abrupt verſe in his mouth, euen dying wouderfully exulted. Another time when the Kingly Prophet, not only conſidered that he was to goe to the houſe of the Lord, but ſending his ſoule as it were before him into thoſe galleryes themſelues and entryes of heauen,

 and

and priuily laying his eares to the doores in a manner of the Nuptial Chamber, and obscurely hearing a kind of whispering (I know not) of some of the ioyes there within, it not only wiped away from him al sadnes, caused in him through the formes exprobration obiected to him of *Where is his God?* but dilating his breast, made him to powre forth his soule into most sweet and extatical pleasures: And wherefore? *Because* (saith he) *I shal enter into the place of the admirable Tabernacle euen to the house of God in the voyce of exultation, and confession, the sound of the Master of the feast.* (h)

Lastly, another time, being yet mortal when creeping by stealth as it were he had secretly insinuated himself into the bowre or conclaue of the immortals, comparing them with himself and our humane affai-

affaires, he brake forth into these termes of ioy, and congratulation: *How louely are thy Tabernacles oh Lord of vertues! my soule couets and longs after the galleries of the Lord My hart and my flesh, haue reioyced in the liuing God. Blessed are they, Lord, who dwel in thy house, they shal praise thee foreuer and euer. Because in thy galleries one day is better then a thousand,* (i] *to wit, so great is the pleasure of the eternal light,* which (S. Augustin, expresly saith in these words (k) *that though it were not lawful to enioy it longer then a day, yet for that only, innumerable yeares of this life, ful of delights and the aboundance of temporal goods, vvere worthily and with reason to be contemned. For it vvas not falsely or slightly said, that better is one day in thy Galleries, then a thousand.* So as it is less to be admired, that *Dauid* should presently adde this also: *I haue chosen rather to be an abiect in the house of my God, then to dvvel in the Tabernacles of sinners.* (l) I had rather, saith he, be in the lowest office of a doore-keeper in the porch of the Temple, and there watch at the entry as a slaue before him, with the hope of enioying this celestial beatitude, then with the hazard of loosing it; in the most ample and sumpteous Palaces and houses, to be obserued and courted, by a number of clyents, and frends. Hence, that affection of the mind aspiringe vnto Heauen with a swift course, *As the Hart, couets the fountaines of vvaters, so my soule desires thee, O God.* (m) That kind of beast truly is fleet and swift, but then flyes he with most speed, when either being chased by hounds, or bitten with serpents, he feeles an extraordinary thirst, for then to quench that heat he runnes headlong to the fountaines, & flyes like

like the winds. *Dauid* thirsted likwise, and no lesse groaned & sighed after heauen. *When shal I come and appeare before the face of God?* And for the great desire he had and loue to the heauenly countrey and the felicity of the Blessed, which euen absent he had tasted now and then, had so great a horrour tediousnes and auersion from humane things, as teares to him were of familiar as bread to others, nor vsed he food more frequently then teares, yea teares themselues were food vnto him; so as oppressed with dolours neither would he take his food, or so much as thinke thereof; while to him thus vehemently thirsting after the presence of God, this gibing taunt was obbrayded to his face, *Where is thy God?*

From al which this same may be gathered, that if in these Galleries, though

though absent *Dauid* and diuers other Saintly men haue taken such pleasure, with what ioyes and delights may we not imagine those to swimme in, who are admitted into the secret closet and cabinet of the Spouse? If but a slight ray onli of the blessed vision, so dazle the eyes of the mind; if but a drop of the water of Paradise and fountaine of the chiefest good but lightly sprinckled; if but a crumme falling from the table of our Lord, so recreates and refresheth mortals, what wil the whole sunne himself doe? what wil the very Ocean of al good things? what wil the table of our Lord himself conferre to the immortals? Shal not the hart euen swimme trow you, in these delights, yea be wholy immersed, and drowned in them.

(a) *Rom.* 8. (b) *Iza.* 58. (c) 2. *Cor.* 12. (d) 3. *Reg.* 10. (a) *S. Bonau.* *in in vita S. Fran.* (f) *Psal.* 56. (g) *Psal.* 111. (h] *Psal.* 41. (i) *Psal.* 83. [k] *Aug. lib.* 3. *de lib. arb. c. vlt.* (l) 1. *Par.* 9. (m] *Psal.* 14.

XX. MEDITATION.

The preparatory Prayer.

Actiones nostras quesumus, &c.

THE PRELVDE.

VV*Hen he shal appeare, we shal be like to him: because we shal see him as he is: And whosoeuer hath this hope in him, sanctifies himself as he is holy.*

1. *Point.* Consider how great a good, how excellent, how delecta-ble it is, most cleere to behold one God in essence, three in Persons, Father, Sonne, and Holy-Ghost; and that eternally in the mirrour of the

the hart: *Surely, the eye hath not seen, nor eare heard, nor hath it ascended into the hart of man what God hath prepared for such as loue him:* (a) Tast with the inward sense these delights of the heauenly Paradise, and loath the leeke, and garlike of *AEgipt* the miry bogs, the empty husks & filthines of the world. Oh if thou couldst but take a tast or assay before hand with the glorious *S. Augustin* of the ioyes of the Blessed, thou wouldst say with him: *How sweet to me sudenly it vvas to vvant those svveets of idly toyes, and vvhat before vvas a griefe to loose vvas novv a ioy to forgoe vvholy thou eiectedst them from me, the true and chiefest svveetnes, and entredst thy self in, insteed of them, svveeter farr then al pleasure.* (b)

2. *Point.* Ponder how, much this same cogitation may and ought auayle to endure and goe through with

with any hart and difficult entreprise for God and our saluation. What changes sudenly and alterations of minds, those fruites wrought whith come from the land of Promise, (c) which made them surmoũt the difficulties, they feared so much before? What doe not the wrastlers generously performe and suffer in sight of the goal and crownes proposed? *Surely the sufferings of this time are not condigne to the future glory, vvhich shalbe reuealed in vs.* (d]With which only napkin, (as S. Gregory obserues (e)] that glorious and illustrious Champion of the Christian lists *S. Paul.* wiped away al the sweat of the infinit and most greeuous labours and troubles he sustained; and so likewise the rest of Martyrs. But this especially when *S. Adrian* being a Soldiours, in the flower of his age, beheld a great number of Christians

ſtians to runne very ioyful and glad into torments , ſcaffolds , gibbets, Croſſes , fires , as it were to a wedding , asked what hope it was that drew & led them to it : and when it was anſwered they hoped for thoſe goods which *the eye hath not ſeen, nor eare heard , nor hath aſcended into the hart of man* , he was ſo mooued and changed therewith , that preſently he gaue vp his name to be put into the liſt , and vnder *Maximian* moſt ſtoutly and valiantly ſuffred Martyrdome. So much the hope of beatitude could worke.

3. *Point.* See how immenſe and powerful is the diuine loue of IESVS , which through grace at laſt leads a man vnto the viſion it-ſelf, of the diuine eſſence , wherewith euen God himſelf is bleſſed. Then thinke what thou oughtſt to yeald to recompence this loue againe : no leſſe

lesse no doubt then reciprocal loue. For when God loues, he would no more then to be loued againe; knowing thẽ who loue him only, to be truly blessed. So *S.Bernard* in his 83. Sermon on the Canticles. But to the end thou maist loue God thou art wholy to empty thy hart from the loue of al other things. *For euen as a vessel* (which is S.Anselmes discourse) *the more water is in it or any other liquour, conteynes lesse oyle; so the more the hart is taken vp with other loues the more it excludeth this. There is yet another, that as stench is contrary to a good odour, and darknes to light, so is al other loue contrarie, to this: As therefore contraries doe neuer agree wel together; so this loue agrees not with any other loue in the hart.*

(a) *Rom.* 8. (b) *Lib* 9. *Conf. cap.* 1. (c) *Num.* 13. (d) *Rom.* 8. (e) *in Iob cap* 7.

THE

THE COLLOQVY.

SHal be made to IESVS, the most deare louer of soules of whom shalt thou earnestly beg, to impart vnto thee his diuine loue which this or the like forme: *My God, giue me thy self; behold I loue thee, and if this be too litle may I loue thee more. I cannot measure how much loue I want, of that which were enough. This know I only, it goes il with me, without thee: and al aboundance which is not my God, is meere pouerty. Let the sweet power then of thy loue deuour me, grant I may liue and dye with the loue of thy loue, since first thou hast so loued, as thou hast not only afforded me and done many great things for me; but hast likewise vouchsafest to dye for me.* (a)

Lastly from the inward bowels, make an act of the loue of God aboue

aboue al things , and ſo conclude in thee wonted manner with a Pater & Aue.

(a) *Ex S. Aug & S. Franciſco.*

AN INCENTIVE

Of the Act of the loue of God aboue al things.

GOod God! thou commaund me to loue thee, and threatneſt if I doe it not: Is there any need of theſe chaynes for me to be tyed to loue thee? Am I ſo voyd of ſenſe, as to be ignorant of thy benefits, graces, perfections? Or rather doe I want a hart, to loue an infinit good? Now if loue be to be recompenced with loue, what loue can parallel the diui-

diuine loue? Thou haſt loued me eternally, euen when I was not or poſſibly could loue thee: Thou haſt created the world, & cõſerueſt it hitherto for my ſake: Thou haſt giuen order to the Angels to guard me: Thou wouldſt be my reward beyond meaſure. Thou calleſt me a ſinner to grace and pennance, But yet is this farre more louely, moſt ſweet Sauiour, that being God, thou wouldſt become man, to ſuffer ſo hard and cruel things and laſtly dye on the Croſſe for me who had (cruel as I am] ſo engaged thee death. But this of al others is moſt ſweet, that being neere to death thou leftſt me thy body and bloud in the Sacrament, an admirable pledge of thy loue towards me. Oh Loue! o extaſis of loue! How thou deſeru'ſt, my God, to be highly loued of al men, aboue al things. May I therefore ſo loue thee

thee (my IESVS ,) Sauiour of louers and loue of Sauiours, and ſo let the face of thy loue euen ſwallow me ; that I may liue and dye with the loue of thy loue, who through the loue of my loue , haſt likwiſe vouchſafed to dye for me. Oh infinit goodnes of God ?

A Formulary of the loue of God aboue al things.

O Great God , I loue thee aboue al things ; I loue thee with al my hart , with al my ſoule , with al my powers, and meerly of this ſame loue I am ſorry aboue al things for offending thee the infinit good: moſt firmely reſoluing hence forth, through thy grace , to keep al thy commandements. And why doe I loue thee aboue al things ? ſurely for this; for thy immenſe perfection, incomcomprehensible power, highest wisdome, infinit sanctity and godnes, that is, for thy self, O Father, O Sonne, O Holy-Ghost three persons, one God, who art aboue al things. Amen. IESVS.

Ad maiorem Dei gloriam.

FINIS.

APPENDIX

Iesus, qui te ſubarrhauit, Nuptiales ſume veſtes.
Nunc in Corde præparauit Tibi ſpōſus iam, cæleſtes
Quas promiſit nuptias. Parauit delicias.

19

Post fel crudū crucis diræ,
Melle voluptatis miræ
Sponsus sponsam reficit.

Cor speculum Deitatis,
Et totius Trinitatis
Obstupet, ac deficit.

20